Antique & Collectible

FISHING RODS

Identification and Value Guide

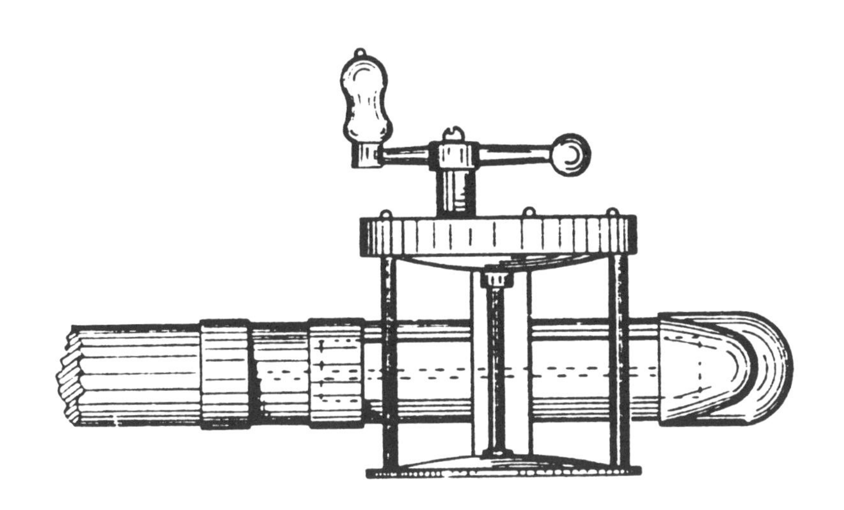

D. B. Homel

Third Printing 2000

The rod values stated herein are the subjective opinion of the author and meant to serve as a basic guideline for the hobby collector. Independent investigation of value and the appraisal of each individual item by an expert is recommended before sale or speculation for profit.

FORREST PARK PUBLISHERS
P. O. Box 29775
Bellingham, Washington 98228
(360) 647-2505

PRINTED IN THE UNITED STATES OF AMERICA

ISBN: 1-879522-07-1

Table of Contents

Acknowledgments

The following individuals provided great assistance in the compilation of text and photographs: Dwight Lyons, Mike Berry, Walt Johnson, John Peterson, Hugh Lewis, George McCabe, Walt Zacharias, George Haymond, and Harold Jellison — many thanks.

Introduction is an excerpt from *The Quiet Pool* — award winning book of short stories by D. B. Homel.

Credits

- Principal Photography — D.B. Homel
- Photographs Pages 64 thru 69 — George W. McCabe
- Top Photograph Page 58 — Mike Malloy
- Supplemental Darkroom Work — Quicksilver
- Electronic Prepress — Cindy Matson

Frontis page: Application drawing of the Fred Devine *Improved Reel Holder and Fastening — For Fishing Rods* (patent granted December 1, 1885).

Introduction

Anglers are indeed tackle nuts. Most own a bundle of rods, at least three or four reels, extra spools, and every conceivable line configuration, gadget and device. And more lures or flies than could be cast in one thousand years.

While new tackle, fresh from the maker's factory, holds some degree of excitement for the majority of consumers — it is tackle from the past that can bring about a serious emotional response from the avid angler.

Why do people collect old fishing tackle? Why do we covet any thing ancient and antique? I contend that it must be *nostalgia* — clearly a yearning for what is perceived to have been a simpler time and probably was. Here lies the heart of the matter. We miss what is past, not necessarily the era in history, but our own childhood. A time when we knew not much and worried little.

Of all things angling, the bamboo rod most strongly represents the past. It is true that these lilting instruments of the lake and stream are still built by hand. A few stalwart craftsmen can yet be found splitting bamboo culms (Tonkin cane) and hand-beveling the thin individual strips, which are glued-up to form a hexagonal blank. When fully adorned and finished the great rod, contemporary though it may be, is worthy of a king's ransom.

Old used bamboo rods are different. Each one seems to have a story to tell — of fish and perhaps a little about the angler who's palm encircled the soiled cork grip. Occasionally the story is known, but usually it is not. New owners, in turn, contribute their part to the ongoing heritage.

I remember some rods, not in a bizarre spiritual way, just fondly. The "Winston" rod is one of these.

About ten years ago it was my pleasure to receive an especially beautiful classic bamboo rod with an interesting history. Being a resident of the Pacific

Northwest, I was logically drawn toward long rods suited to fishing in a brisk wind or on big, open water. This golden hued rod was long and light, a combination of attributes not always associated with cane.

By correspondence with a dealer in Georgia, I was able to purchase the early, Stoner built Winston tucked in the original bag and labeled aluminum tube. It arrived encumbered with a bit of disrepair, having rusted guides and a loose ferrule. However, at nine feet and exhibiting a delicate tip, it might cast a seven weight line with great ease. The old varnish smelled like forty seasons of opening days. And the price was right!

The rod was first owned by the late author, Henry Bruns, who wrote me a letter after learning it had come into my possession. Evidently Hank had used the rod for "research" while gathering information about trout fishing in Northern California, Oregon, and Washington. His assignment was to draft a travel article for *Sunset Magazine* and the rod was found to be ideal for subduing big resident rainbows, coastal cutthroat, and steelhead along the way. In fact, he procured the rod directly form the legendary Lew Stoner at his San Francisco Shop. Although Stoner was apparently hard of hearing, Bruns was able to communicate his needs well enough. By the tone of his letter to me, I learned of his affection for this rod.

I liked the rod too, but was afraid to actually fish it, since the rough guides would tear-up a good fly line and the loose male ferrule would surely damage the bamboo itself. For five years I procrastinated about having it professionally refinished, hesitant to alter the original character and patina. Finally, as Mr. Bruns himself had done, I parted with it — in a trade for a smaller Orvis trout rod.

Months later I got a call from Dwight Lyons, a friend and expert rod restorer in Portland. The Winston had been sent to Dwight who had somehow found a spool of old guide wrapping silk that was an exact match. He then refinished the rod to original specifications.

Dwight's words still ring in my ear: "Dan, why didn't you keep that rod"!

I should have.

Fishing Rod Materials

Ancient indigenous peoples and early settlers in many parts of the world, where fishing was an economic and life sustaining necessity, are known to have fashioned crude angling rods and apparatus from tree limbs, culms of cane, and available vegetable forms. Fishing lines and nets were crafted from horse tail-hair, silk, and woven plant materials. Native peoples of the Pacific Northwest Salish cultures created fishing long lines from the stringy stalk of nettle bushes.

The refined art of building rods specifically for sport fishing was developed in Western Europe prior to the time of the legendary Isaac Walton and his classic book *The Complete Angler* (1654). Anglers of Walton's day utilized cumbersome 15 foot rods made of lance or greenheart wood, and were resolved to lashing rod sections together with twine at a splice in the joints.

Poaching was prevalent in Britain during the 18th century, where "experts" often recommended a rod of eight to twelve pieces which could be concealed in a top coat. Some wood poacher's rods were designed to be hidden in a walking stick.

WOOD RODS

Although most early rods were constructed entirely of wood, evidence indicates that stiff wood butt sections were sometimes combined with tip sections of more flexible materials such as Calcutta bamboo or baleen (whale bone). Rod makers continued to experiment with the natural, organic substances available from both local and imported sources.

During the mid-19th century, rod making moved a giant leap forward with the advent of true ferrules, functional reel seats, and better rod tapers. Fishing, for some, became more than just "dabbling" a line tied to the end of the rod. Integration with the reel was imperative, and the balance of rod and reel was now worthy of great consideration. It was due, in part, to the relationship between rod and reel that rods for different types of fishing were developed.

British rod makers seemed to favor greenheart wood for high grade fly and casting rods. This strong, fine-grained and flexible material produced a rod with a soft pleasant action and fair power. A well made, ten foot greenheart trout rod would make an excellent fishing tool even today — so it is understandable why many British and Eastern Canadian makers continued to round this wood into rod blanks as late as the 1930s.

American made wood rods were constructed of native hickory and ash, along with the greenheart and lance woods. Wood bait rods of the Civil War era resembled a long billiard cue stick and might display a grip made of tightly wound rattan that is varnished. Tiny nickel-silver "trumpet" or "tunnel" style guides were fastened to the wood shaft with dark silk or stout cotton thread.

Charles F. Orvis began to produced the venerable "Henshall" style bait rod around 1884. It was inspired by the recommendations of Dr. James Henshall in his article entitled *The Coming Black Bass Rod* published in the February, 1875 issue of Forest and Stream. In following Henshall's suggestions, Orvis made the ideal bass rod constructed of an ash butt, lancewood "second joint", and lancewood tips at a total length of 8 feet and 3 inches with standing guides — and the reel seat affixed above the hand grip.

Thomas H. Chubb of Post Mills, Vermont sold "first class" lancewood fly rods complete with ferrule plugs for a mere $4.00 in 1886. The 10 1/2 foot Chubb rod came nestled in a cedar wood form case equipped with two tips and enclosed in a heavy canvas bag.

A testimonial to the popularity of greenheart is evident in the offerings of the Montague Rod and Reel Company in 1938. At that time, the company advertised boat and casting rods constructed of turned maple and degame woods that were stained to imitate greenheart.

Hickory wood rods for big game trolling were marketed by Montague and Edward Vom Hofe as late as 1940. However, no other natural rod material has endured or been more highly desired than split bamboo.

SPLIT BAMBOO RODS

The search for a rod material of strength, resiliency, and relative light weight led to the practice of splitting, planing, and gluing bamboo (cane). While early English rod makers originated this craft, perfection and significant advancement in the art of constructing rods made entirely of bamboo is universally credited to the American artisan.

Although there has been considerable debate on the subject, it is generally thought that Samuel Phillipe of Pennsylvania was the first American to produce a split bamboo rod.

In 1871, an outdoorsman and gunsmith named Hiram Leonard designed and built his first fishing rod of ash and lancewood in Bangor, Maine. Soon he was producing four-strip bamboo rods of Calcutta. These early Calcutta rods were sold to the sporting goods retailer Bradford & Anthony of Boston and had a mottled appearance when compared to later, Tonkin cane rods. Leonard subsequently adapted a six-strip principle (60 degree bevels to form the whole hexagonal blank) to his rod operation and thus was born the first commercial bamboo rod as we know it today.

Hiram Leonard started the first American rod factory in Central Valley, New York during 1881. Pioneer rod makers Payne, Thomas, Edwards, and Hawes all apprenticed at the Leonard factory. Of course, these craftsmen eventually left their own marks on the rod making trade as history would unfold. Several taught their sons the rod makers art. Unlike Leonard himself, they would have the benefit of working with lighter and better quality Tonkin cane — from which a vast new array of complex and efficient taper designs could be achieved.

Later western makers such as E.C. Powell and Lew Stoner (Winston) experimented with hollow construction techniques to make bamboo rods even lighter. Creative experimentation with the bamboo rod was not a novel idea. Hardy Brothers of England marketed “steel-centre” bamboo rods during the early 20th century while their competitor, Fosters, laid claim to a stronger product — the “steel-ribbed” rod. Both exhibit abominable actions. Of course, let us not forget the rather odd Devine bamboo rods, sold by retailers such as Abercrombie & Fitch, with their eight strips, “twisted” construction, or blanks wrapped the entire length with transparent silk!

Mass production took the bamboo rod market by storm. Fast, modern operations and automated milling machines allowed for the introduction of many rod styles and lengths at reasonable prices. A handmade fly rod from the E.F. Payne Company sold for $50 in 1930 — at the same time a mass produced Montague "Mt. Tom" could be had for three bucks.

After World War Two, Orvis introduced its famous bakelite impregnated rods. A natural bamboo product with a little synthetic technology thrown in! The Orvis company also contributed advancements in gluing techniques with synthetic cement. The Colorado rod maker, Bill Phillipson, sold many durable resin impregnated rods during the 1960s — as did Sharpes, Sealey, and Farlow of Britain.

Though this chapter is intended to be a brief historical account of rod materials, rather than rod makers, it might still be considered heresy not to mention praiseworthy craftsmen of the post World War Two period. Individual makers such as Paul Young, Mr. Dickerson, Everett Garrison, and Jim Payne (son of E.F. Payne) meticulously rendered their original designs with traditional charm and elegance. The fine fishing instruments they produced are the standard by which contemporary cane rods are judged.

STEEL RODS

As interest in sport fishing spread through North America during the early part of the 20th century, the average angler had neither the time nor inclination to care for an expensive bamboo rod. The steel rod provided a practical, workhorse fishing tool produced from a fabricated material — the true precursor to fiberglass and graphite. The arrival of steel rods on the fishing scene was certainly a foreboding event for the traditionalist, and a boon to the industry.

The Horton Manufacturing Company of Bristol Connecticut was the leader in tubular steel rod design and distribution. Many of the pivotal, early patents (1887-1912) pertaining to steel blank construction, ferrule integration, telescopic function, and reversible handles were held by Horton. In the April, 1918 issue of *Field and Stream* , Horton advertised the "Bristol" steel fishing rods in prices ranging from $3.50 to $25.00 and noted that they could be bought in 16,000 stores. L.M.

Richardson of Chicago, a competitor in the steel rod trade and a maker of the well-known collapsible nets, offered steel fly rods with a genuine agate stripper and tip-top for only $3.00 each during the same year ($2.00 with no agates — a real bargain!)

Most steel rod manufacturers produced tubular steel rods for fly and bait fishing along with shorter, solid alloy steel casting rods for use with multiplying reels. Beryllium copper was another material which was later used to construct fresh water bait casting as well as salt water rods. The American Fork & Hoe Co. of Geneva, Ohio specialized in selling one piece solid steel rods for bait casting called the "True Temper". The taper of the rod was hand ground and the steel was tempered by an electrical heat treatment which rendered a stout fishing tool capable of hauling-in the largest species.

Beginning in 1932, Winchester marketed a line of steel rods with a painted-on bamboo finish. Heddon followed this practice, and got so carried away in promoting these "bamboo" finish steel rod that their ads compared the steel rod's action to that of split bamboo. Without hesitation, most anglers who have tried fishing with old steel rods can attest to their inferior qualities. However, I must admit that a few of the tubular steel "Gep" fly rods made by Gephart Mfg. Co. in the 1940s were so incredibly good that they could function just fine as light trout rods today.

The steel rod phenomena began to fade, not coincidentally when fiberglass technology moved forward after World War Two.

FIBERGLASS RODS

As is the case with steel rods, tubular fiberglass construction is superior to that of the solid glass rod. Solid fiberglass blanks such as the "Lexon" brand were less time consuming and cheaper to make than tubular blanks. Most were composed of glass fibers packed solid in resin, baked and then ground to the desired shape.

Typical, tubular fiberglass rods were made of woven or criss-cross fiberglass cloth which was rolled upon a steel mandrel and impregnated with plastic resins to form the desired taper and blank-wall thickness — thus the different actions and rod sizes could be achieved. Some of the most appealing fiberglass rods of this type from the 1950s are those made on the famous, rich golden-brown "Silaflex" blanks. Early fiberglass rod ferrules were carried over from bamboo rod making, and are commonly found to be nickel-plated brass, aluminum, and occasionally nickel-silver.

Shakespeare of Kalamazoo, Michigan was an innovator in tubular fiberglass rod technology. Armed with the patented "Howald Process" they developed a wide variety of casting, trolling, spinning, and fly rods in the 1960s and 1970s called *Wonderods.* The "Howald Process" incorporated thousands of individual glass fibers running parallel, the full length of the rod. Shakespeare claimed this produced a blank with more precise wall thickness resulting in a rod with better action and control.

Some of the best fiberglass fly and spinning rods came from the Phillipson factory in Denver, Colorado. Phillipson "Epoxite" rods were derived from 3M Company's longitudinal fiberglass cloth, and cured under exceptional pressure. The resulting rod had an extraordinary strength to weight ratio and remarkable action. The first Phillipson rods sported nickel-silver ferrules, while later rods were fitted with glass to glass ferrules.

Orvis, Hardy, R.L. Winston, and H.L. Leonard companies, names synonymous with fine bamboo rods, sold outstanding fiberglass fly rods made of "full-length" (longitudinal fibers), high density glass. Often the reel seat, and other components were equivalent to the maker's best bamboo rods.

Before fiberglass fell-from-grace and was pushed aside by the graphite revolution, several noteworthy mass-produced rods were to be enjoyed by hordes of anglers. The best of the lot, many of which are still in use today, came from Fenwick (patented "Feralite" rods) and Garcia (Conolon blanks).

Close-up of a Heddon steel rod with the painted, simulated bamboo finish

Early Wright & McGill fiberglass fly rod exhibiting woven-cloth construction

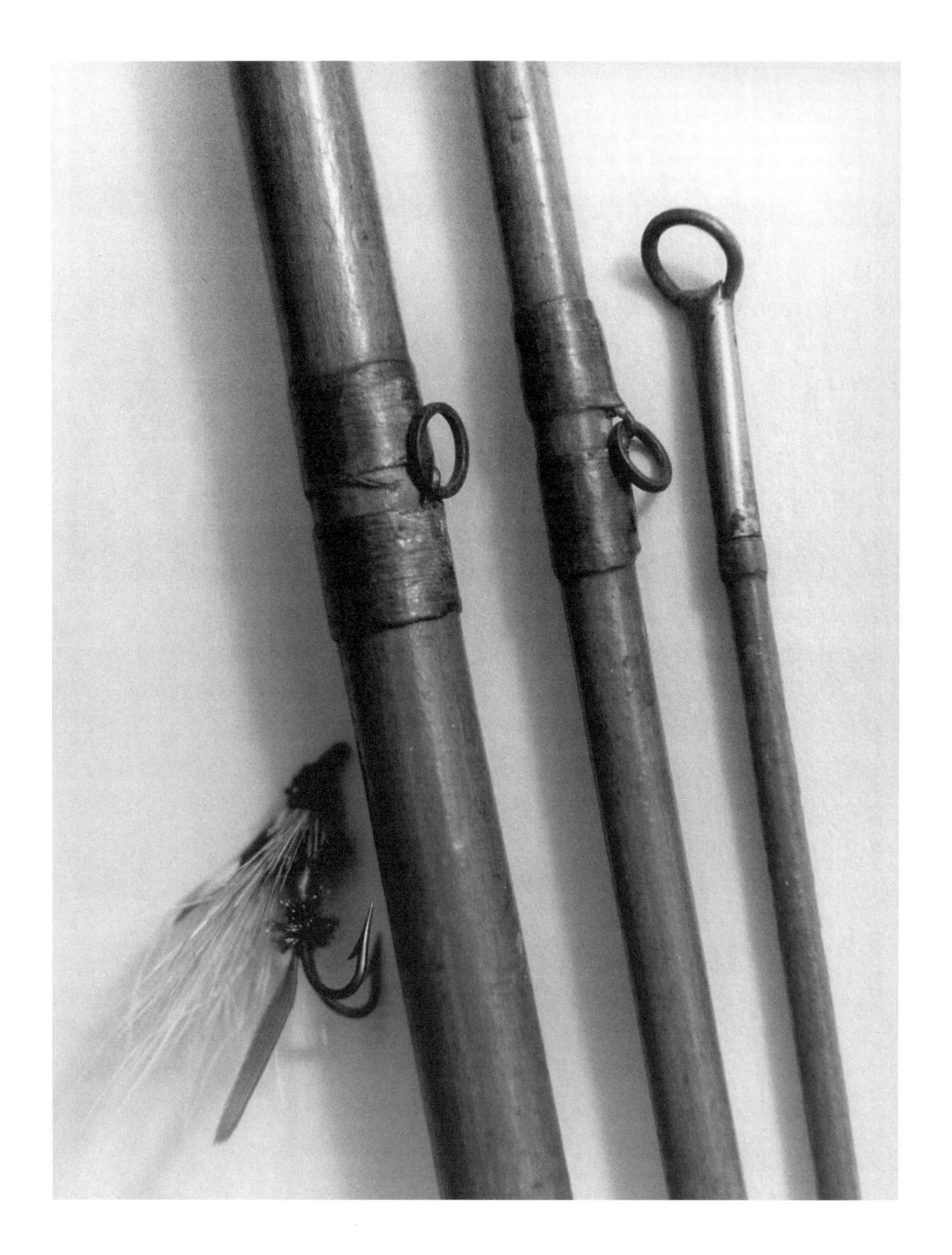

Greenheart wood fly rod circa 1885 with the original flip-ring guides

Evaluation

Ask any rod collector how many times they have experienced the following scenario . . .

Arriving at the barn sale, I was ushered into a damp, dusty corner below the loft, by an old fellow with a moth eaten fly in his hat.

"Haven't fished these rods in twenty years — got one of 'em from my dad", the old man grumbled. "Fishin's not worth a damn any more, so I might as well sell 'em".

The gambrel style barn smelled like alfalfa and antiques. It felt promising! Other "early birds" were walking up the path, as I began unscrewing the cap on the first of three rod tubes. They were all long tubes, certainly fly rods. Two of the tubes had the word *Heddon* engraved in the top of the cap. The other was missing its label, but the cap was brass, indicative of perhaps a Leonard or Thomas. Each tube was marked with a price of $25. The first rod was indeed a Leonard, a nine foot Tournament model that looked to be in pretty good condition — except for a minor repair wrap to a hook-dig on one tip. The old guy had used this one only a dozen times, I thought to myself. He had spent more time talking about fishing, than actually wetting a line.

I looked over my shoulder, and recognized another local collector at the entrance to the barn. Not bothering to inspect the two Heddons, I quickly pulled seventy-five bucks from my wallet, paid the old grouch, and walked past my envious competitor with the rods tucked securely under my arm. On the way home I almost drove off the road as I glanced over at the rods leaning against the front seat.

At home, I discovered that the two Heddons were virtually unfished, modest #14 rods — all original down to the price marked on the tag sewn to the partitioned cloth bag.

Then I woke up! Hell, it was only a dream.

More likely the real life scenario would entail being scooped by the other collector or finding the rods to be in total disrepair. But we keep looking, searching, and hoping to uncover yet another interesting old rod. When we find it, the potential purchase must be ferruled together, flexed, and examined. We now must decide whether it is worth the asking price, or for that matter worth messing with at any price.

The following system has been developed, over many years, for analyzing the condition of collectible fishing rods. It has served this writer well, and I hope it is helpful to the reader. If you are inexperienced with fishing rods and your intent is to evaluate a rod for the purpose of sale, perhaps this chapter will enlighten you — or at least rebuff the myth that . . . *if it's old and a bamboo rod, then it's absolutely worth big money.*

(1) ORIGINAL PACKAGING

A fishing rod, especially a split bamboo rod, is very delicate. The tips are finely tapered and easily broken. Consequently, the original protective tube and bag were an integral part of the outfit. The rod was stored and transported in the tube. Most high quality bamboo fly and spinning rods, some casting rods, and a few steel rods were originally sold enclosed in a partitioned bag and tube. Tubes were often aluminum, but were also constructed of leather, fiber (cardboard) material, and bamboo. Many casting rods and some larger fly rods were packaged in a heavy canvas sack, fitted with a long wood dowel for support and protection. Still other rods, including older greenheart, hickory wood and Calcutta bamboo salmon rods were provided with a canvas sack and slender aluminum or hollow bamboo "tip tube" for storage of the most fragile section — the tip (or tips). Early twentieth century bamboo trout rods were often sold nestled in a cedar form case or a case of lesser wood covered in felt. Numerous production rods, or economy rods were sold with a light bag only.

Because the case (tube) and/or bag was so important to the rod, collectors prefer and seek out rods in this original packaging. It is a fact that a collectible rod is devalued when the original case, tube, or bag is missing.

A modern or non-original tube (or bag) accompanying an older, classic rod can also create doubt as to the rod's originality. At first blush, a modern tube with an old rod raises the presumption of a refinish or restoration job — a state of condition which is less desirable than an original, unaltered rod. It is, of course, possible that an unaltered rod found its way into a newer tube. Perhaps the owner mixed-up his rods after fishing or lost a cap and decided to replace the whole tube. In any event, look closely at such a rod with suspicion.

(2) INTEGRITY OF THE BLANK

The rod blank or shaft; upon which the guides, tip-top, reel seat, and ferrules (if any) are placed, is the heart of the instrument. It is the most difficult and costly portion to replace. Often, the cost to rebuild one split bamboo tip alone will exceed the market value of the entire collectible rod. In the case of steel and fiberglass rods, the task of searching-out or fabricating a broken section is hardly worth the effort.

A problem with any part of the rod blank can alert the collector to a lack of structural integrity. Although many collectible rods are displayed, hoarded, and pampered — it is the idea that they "could be fished" which drives prices higher on better quality rods. If it can't stand up to actual casting or fishing, it is less valuable, period.

Short tips are frequently encountered in bamboo rods, particularly those delicate fly rods used for trout fishing. A fast action or so-called dry fly rod will likely be broken near the top, while a slower, parabolic rod may be severed further down toward the ferrule. Of course, the location of the break depends on whether the rod was damaged during casting, "short-bending" while playing a fish, or careless transportation to and from the water. Rods were commonly stepped-on at stream-side and slammed in car doors.

Breaks are also noticeable at the ferrules. Check the rod to make sure all sections are full length. Occasionally, two piece rods are encountered with a staggered ferrule design where the tip section is made longer than the butt section. In this case, measure the rod's total length as indicated on the rod shaft, tube, or bag.

Breaks are not always complete. A splinter or fracture in bamboo may be repairable. Such restoration work is best saved for an expert if the rod is worthwhile and of high quality. If the fracture is in the tip, and the rod is accompanied by an extra tip, the rod may still be valuable. Again, the cost to repair or replace the extra tip may exceed the worth gained by having a rod with two tips. Further, the rod would have one repaired or replaced tip — and could not be appraised at the same value level as a rod with two original, unaltered tips.

Most split bamboo rods are constructed of six beveled strips, glued-up to form a hexagonal blank. Delamination of the beveled bamboo strips at the glue lines can create a major problem that will necessitate a costly restoration job. Any rod bearing such an affliction must be considered in poor condition.

One of the more acceptable structural flaws found in rods is a set or "bend" in the blank. Steel rods with a bend have been physically abused, and careful rebending may remedy the problem. In contrast, bamboo rods can acquire a set or "bow" from storage! A slight tip-set is minor, and may not greatly effect value. If the tip-set just about circles around and looks you right in the eye, it is something to be examined more closely. Moisture may have crept into the material and caused a deeper problem.

When the rod is put together, look to see if the top-section or mid-section extends straight-out from the male ferrule. If the section is crooked, the problem may be at the ferrule. A sophisticated repair may be in order, requiring a removal and re-set of the ferrule itself.

Hook-digs, deep scratches, line gouges, and dings are often covered with a clear silk repair wrap. This will cause a reduction in value when the rod is otherwise in excellent condition. It is expected, but not favored, in a rod at the "fair" or "good" level. Keep a sharp eye for repair wraps, mate — for they may conceal such grievous defects as fractures, poorly executed splices and the like!

(3) DAMAGED OR REPLACED PARTS

Excessive wear or damage to cork grip, reel seat, guides, tip-top, hook-keeper, or ferrules is relatively obvious. A thorough inspection should reveal the degree of damage or wear, and the appraisal of over-all condition should be adjusted accordingly. Replaced parts are a different story — and are not so easily recognized. A slick restoration job may be discovered only upon notice of subtle component inconsistencies. But first let us address damage and wear.

Cork, wood, or rattan grips are sometimes encountered in varying degrees of distress. Chunks of cork are often chipped away (from embedding hook, fly or lure thereto), rattan can be tattered, and wood scratched. More often the problem is not so much damage as it is years of dirt, old varnish, or a sorry attempt by the seller to refurbish.

Ferrules are a more important concern. Watch out for loose ferrules — loose where the ferrule is attached to the rod blank. Better quality bamboo rod ferrules (nickel silver, or brass on some older rods) were pinned or connected by a method superior to simple gluing. Often it is not a matter of just re-gluing these, but a formidable task made more complex by the need to carefully remove the pin. Once again, this is one of those jobs better left to the professional rod craftsman. As a collector be aware that loose ferrules devalue a rod. If you are a fledgling rod aficionado ask an experienced angler or collector to show you the proper technique for assembling and pulling-apart a ferruled rod. This will help minimize ferrule wear and damage to collectible rods in your possession.

Corrosion can be a problem on metal ferrules, as can hairline cracks. Older ferrules have seams, a likely place to look for cracks. Another problem is a ferrule that is too tight or too loose — a difficulty easily fixed by one skilled at restoration. Still it is a problem to consider.

Reel seats are found made of wood, nickel silver, aluminum, nickel plated brass, cork, bakelite and celluloid. Make sure the mechanism, whether it be sliding band, screw lock, or rings functions properly without a hitch and is firmly in place. Try to spot repaired, soldered cracks in reel seat hoods and sliding bands. Rubber butt caps on boat rods and salmon fly rods are often cracked from age, or are missing. Fighting or extension butts were sometimes misplaced by the angler. Look at the bottom of the handle to see if there is a provision for such a device.

Guides were commonly replaced when a rod was refinished. Only experience will help you determine whether or not the guides are original. If the rod is antique vintage, the original guides would surely be of the "flip-ring", nickel-silver tunnel, or heavy snake style. Many older casting rods came equipped with fine agate-filled guides. Beware of replaced guides. A 90 year old rod with gleaming, new guides wrapped-on in fluorescent hot orange thread and thick epoxy finish is **not** particularly pleasing to the eye. Unfortunately more and more fine rods are ruined by this well-intended but foolish act. More on this later.

Tip-top guides were commonly replaced due to wear, or in the event of a break. The larger diameter at the "lower" position on the blank often necessitated the use of a larger, non-original tip-top. A worse scenario occurred when the repair person "shaved-off" some of the blank material in order to utilize the original tip-top guide — thus weakening the tip. Many rods are discovered with two tips — each having a completely different tip-top guide. In this situation, it is fairly obvious that one is an impostor, although some spin/fly and fly/casting combination rods were originally fitted with two different tip section and consequently two different styles of tip-top guide. An incorrect or replaced tip-top guide does not cause irreparable harm, nor does it effect the rod's value to a great degree. It may, however, alert the potential buyer to a more severe defect such as a short tip or non-original tip section.

Missing parts, especially guides, are a common problem. Quite a few guides have been broken off by angler and collector alike, due to a hasty shove into the rod's aluminum tube. Always cup your hand around the mouth of the tube. As you lower the rod into the tube, let the protruding guides rub against your hand instead of the sharp, hard edge of the tube top.

Is a missing rod part always obvious? Not when we are talking about extra tips for fly rods. Policies varied from year to year, especially in the marketing of mass produced rods. Some years a certain economy model might be offered with an extra tip — some years not. Many British rods were sold with only one tip. Older Winston, and several Orvis fly rods had only one tip. If the original bag in which the rod came is partitioned, count the slots to determine whether a tip section is missing.

Bamboo baitcasting rods were fairly inconsistent with regard to extra tips. Some were sold with two identical tips, others with a heavy and light tip, however most came equipped with a single tip. Again, if the original bag is included, count the partitions.

(4) COSMETIC APPEARANCE

Be alert to the condition of a rod's cosmetic appearance. Things to look out for in a bamboo rod include originality of the entire rod and finish, cracked or "crazed" varnish, "soft" varnish, and frayed or brittle guide (and intermediate) windings or "wraps".

Some rod collectors are picky about the originality of a rod. If the rod is refinished, even by a skilled rod restorer, they consider this a major flaw. Most would, however, accept a rod that had been refinished by its original maker provided the work can be documented by receipt or correspondence. Since "all-original" rods in the higher grades of condition are becoming tougher to find, the majority of collectors and anglers now seem more willing to embrace quality collectible rods that have been professionally re-finished. In my opinion, these rods still take a back seat to authentic, clean, unaltered rods with their original packaging — and always will. It is therefore important to recognize a refinish when you see it, so that you don't pay too much for what the seller may believe to be an original finish.

Missing decals, removed model numbers on the rod butt, "new looking" guide windings, "new looking", heavy, or sloppy varnish, and mis-matched winding colors are possible clues to a refinish. Many bamboo rods were given one or several over-coats of varnish by their original owners. Varnish which has overlapped the cork grip or ferrules may provide a clue. An over-varnish is a subtle flaw, but worthy of a slight reduction in value. We must remember that touch-up or periodic revarnishing was a necessary part of good rod maintenance and, in fact, may have helped to preserve the rod through many seasons of angling. A fine, extra coat of varnish carefully applied by the owner long ago can be looked upon as a mark of honor.

A rod may be perfect in every way, with the exception of a poor original finish. Many old rods are discovered with varnish that has simply gone soft as a result of age, heat exposure, or exposure to fly floatants and line dressings. Though it may be the original varnish, soft varnish is a really horrible problem because the rod just doesn't "feel" right. The blank feels tacky and often has bag marks or bits of fuzz from the fabric it was stored against.

Cracked or so-called *crazed* varnish is an important defect that can be quite noticeable and displeasing. This malady is also referred to as *alligatored* varnish — since the defect looks like the amphibian's skin. If the condition has not spread to a great degree, the rod may still be quite acceptable, albeit subject to close scrutiny by the experienced collector. Cracked varnish can also be an indicator of water damage, improper storage, or over-varnish — so watch out.

Some bamboo rods were bakelite impregnated. Instead of varnish, the bamboo was soaked in a solution formulated to seal-out moisture and provide great durability. Occasionally, one of these rods will be found with a varnish over-coat. Of course this is not original to the rod and would cause a reduction in value.

Dried-out, brittle guide windings and intermediates are easily recognized because the guide is breaking through at its foot, or the silk has frayed and unraveled. Often the windings will be intact yet weak. Such a condition always raises the dilemma of whether or not to have the rod refinished. It is my opinion that the rod should be **left alone** if it is an antique or collectible that is **not** intended to be fished. Should an angler/collector desire utility from the tired instrument and yearn to cast it upon babbling brook, a refinish might be practical. Make no mistake that an altered or refinished bamboo rod will increase in utility value, but not always in collectible (dollar) value. In fact, a well-meaning but crummy refinish can completely destroy the dollar value of a good bamboo rod. Keep this in mind when selecting a craftsman to do the work.

Steel rods were often painted by the factory in black, brown, or green enamel finish. Look for original paint on the shaft. These rods also accumulated rust at the ferrules and guides, particularly in telescoping models and were routinely repainted. A common defect in steel rods is the incidence of replaced agate guides. The original guide may be wholly incorporated or welded to the steel shaft, while the replacement is crudely affixed by wire, thread or solder. A botched type of repair job such as this will render the average steel rod worthless.

No matter what type of rod you are dealing with, a missing or obliterated decal or model number (usually found on the butt section, above the fore-grip) is a disappointing circumstance. The rod may still be identified due to other distinguishing features (such as an engraved reel seat) however much of the charm may be lost if that particular rod is known to have had a decal or inked markings. It is obvious that most rod traders and dealers consider this to be important. Would you be more interest in rod advertisement (A) or (B)?

> (A) Montague Fishkill 8 1/2′ (3/2) well-used, but in very good condition with a perfect original decal on the shaft.
>
> (B) Unmarked 8 1/2′ (3/2) fly rod most certainly a Montague, probably a Fishkill model. Very good condition.

It is clear that the price for rod (A) would be justifiably higher, possibly double the price of rod (B) and worth it. Further, as I have already suggested, an unmarked rod is the first hint of an amateur refinish job — and a glaring beacon of caution. If you are offered rod (B), put the money back in your wallet unless the asking price is a bargain!

(5) COLLECTING TRENDS

Trends in rod collecting are not so much major shifts in interest as they are traditional tastes which become more profound as time moves forward and the most popular rods become more scarce. However scarcity is not always the deciding issue.

Since the 1960s, classic bamboo fly rod aficionados have coveted shorter instruments "under eight and one half feet" long. These smaller and lighter trout rods seem to be the most "fishable" and practical rods for modern use. We have become accustomed to using rods under 4 ounces in weight. Fiberglass introduced us to this convenience and graphite has certainly taken things one step further. Though many collectors say they intend to fish a collectible or antique rod, most never do. However, it is the **possibility** that the rod is "fishable" which piques the collector's interest — and it is simply more possible and comfortable to fish a bamboo rod that is eight feet, or better yet seven feet in length!

Another, but less significant, factor driving the smaller trout rod's popularity is *low supply*. People often crave objects that are hard to get. Individual makers, as well as production-line rod manufacturers marketed a preponderance of nine foot fly rods. Shorter rods were produced in lower numbers. Combine the low original supply with all the short rods currently hoarded by collectors and the state of affairs is clear.

Quality of the rod has always played a role in the collecting hobby. Hand made rods, rods with better components, rods with finer tapers, and rods by individual makers have been consistently more sought after by experienced, hard core collectors than rods by a production-line manufacturer. In recent years, with the growing battalion of fly rod enthusiasts, these "production rods" have been seen in a different light. Fly rods by Shakespeare, South Bend, H & I, and Montague are becoming the heart of the hobby — because, for many people they are the **only** affordable and available old rods.

Bamboo fly rods produced by Orvis, Heddon, Phillipson, and Granger have found a heightened respect from experienced rod collectors. Although these rods have always been considered superior to the aforementioned mass-produced rods, they never caused much real excitement in the hobby. Times have changed! As more and more angler/collectors discover the quality and performance of fly rods such as the Orvis *Battenkill,* Heddon *Black Beauty,* Phillipson *Peerless,* and Granger *Aristocrat,* their popularity will continue to soar.

Historic, antique fly rods (90 years old or more) of Calcutta bamboo or wood (greenheart for example) are eagerly sought by rod collectors, anglers, decorators, and folk art collectors. Most are long, slow (so-called "wet fly") action rods. Though seldom fished, these nostalgic museum pieces make great wall displays and are relatively low priced, particularly if one is not too concerned about condition.

Bamboo casting and spinning rods are another growing area of the hobby. Although these rod types are becoming more difficult to find in better condition, prices are still reasonably low when compared to a fly rod by the same maker.

Bamboo and hickory boat rods, and more importantly, big game rods should be given a second look by the present day collector. Most of these rods were fished hard, and abused by exposure to salt water. It would be wise to grab any examples you find in "minty" condition.

Steel rods have never been favored by collectors. They are considered too heavy and clumsy for modern tastes, and are less alluring than bamboo rods of the same era. Steel rods are the most common type of old rod encountered at garage sales, swap meets, and antique malls. Does familiarity breed contempt — you bet it does! However, do not disregard the collectible potential of early telescoping or sectioned steel rods by South Bend, Bristol, Richardson and the like. Many of these well made antiques are engraved with historic and significant patent dates. Some are equipped with quality agate guides and tip-tops. Although they are not particularly valuable when compared to bamboo rods, steel rods provide a curious link in the progression and advancement of rod materials and design.

Early fiberglass fly rods are now becoming old enough to be considered collectible. Top quality fiberglass rods make fine angling tools that rival the modern graphite rod in performance. Of course, "glass" rods are slower and softer and may not cast as far — But distance is not everything! Many veteran fly fishers prefer the smooth, parabolic tapers which are prevalent in good fiberglass fly rods. Consequently, the best fiberglass trout rods of the 1960s and 1970s produced by Phillipson, Winston, Orvis, Leonard, and Russ Peak are gaining stature as modern day collectibles and fishables. Even the venerable and numerous Fenwick rods are being pursued by the angler/collector. Much of this stems from utility value since the cost of a new, high quality fly rod is so high. For this reason cheap, mass-produced fiberglass fly rods with poor components and design are **not** worth a heck of a lot.

Old tubular or solid fiberglass casting and boat rods are becoming more nostalgic, but have yet to become valuable. Some light fiberglass spinning rods produced on high quality blanks (Silaflex, Conolon, Fullflex, Fibalite etc.) make excellent fishing tools. The best of the lot were produced or marketed by up-scale companies such as Orvis, Hardy, and Phillipson.

A replaced "double hole" tip-top guide showing evidence of wear and pitting

Hairline cracks in a ferrule (bamboo rod) and metal winding check hardware (wood rod) offer good examples of defects which may greatly reduce both value and utility. Notice also the corrosion of the nickel plating on these parts.

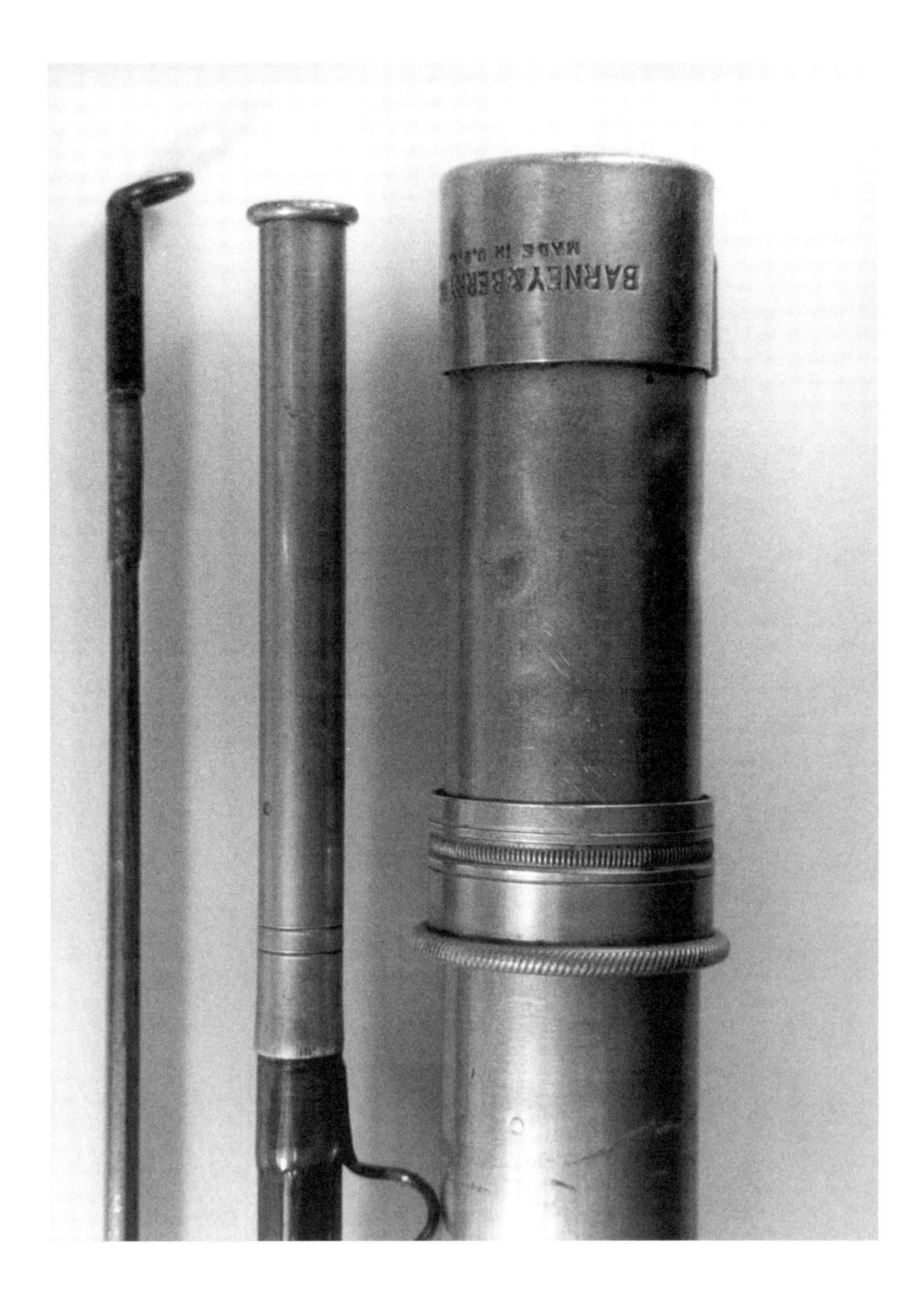

This Barney & Berry bamboo fly rod circa 1915 is well made as evidenced by the nickel-silver ferrule and ornate silver reel seat, both pinned to secure them to the blank. Barney & Berry was the predecessor of Winchester's rod shop supervised by Eustis Edwards. Unfortunately, the rod has been poorly refinished — notice the thick, epoxy coated guide windings. The small dings and scratches in the reel seat are less significant. As a whole, upon evaluation the rod can only be graded in poor-fair condition since it is also missing one tip and is lacking any bag or case.

A bundle of bamboo fishing rods at a garage sale. Does anything decent lurk amongst this pile of junk? You never know!

Fly Rods

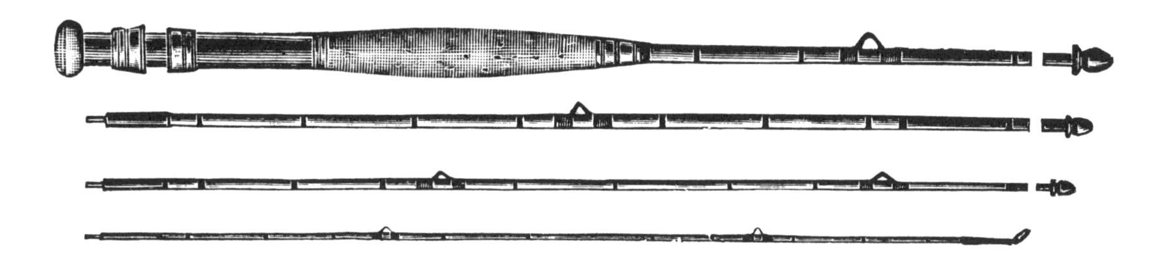

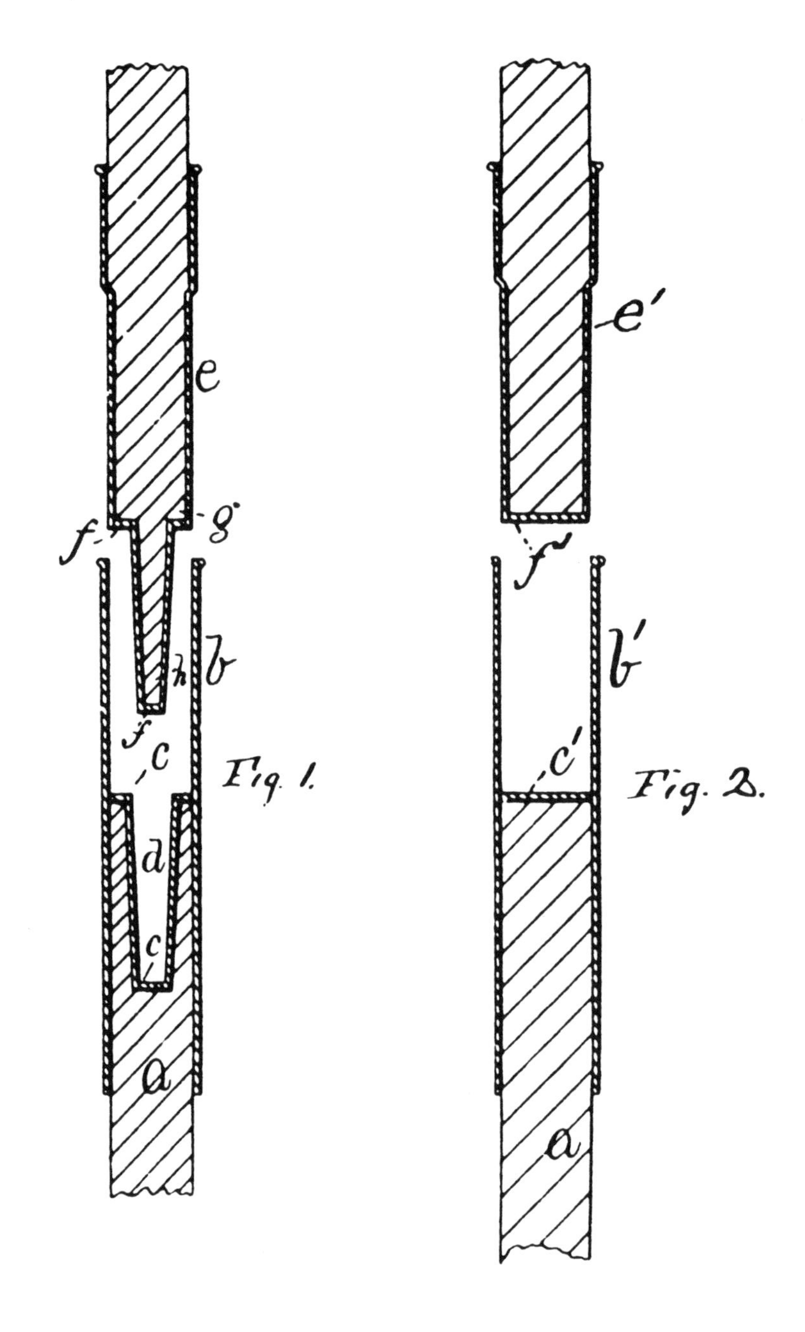

The famous H.L. Leonard patent for a waterproof rod ferrule design. The important engineering feature depicted as part **C** (in figure **2**) is a stop on the inside of the female section covering the end of the wood portion of the rod. This prevented water from penetrating into the wood or cane blank. The waterproof design was particularly important in early split-bamboo rods because any invasive moisture could dissolve the fragile, animal based glues of the time. Figure **1** represents the same function on the older "spiked style" ferrules. No doubt, more work was required to fit the spiked ferrules to the blank.

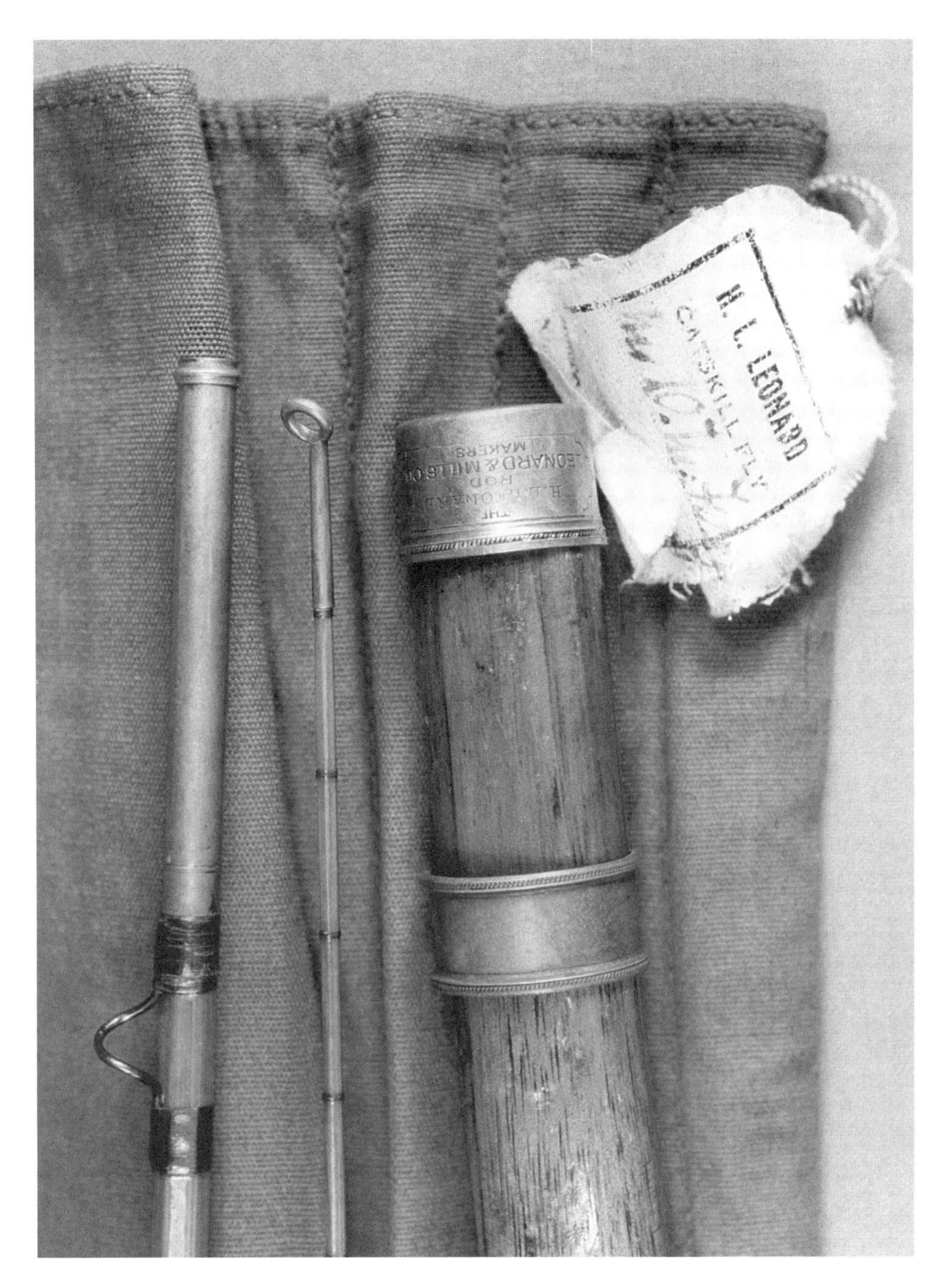

H.L. Leonard *Catskill Fly* trout rod 9 1/2 feet long (3 piece with two tips) sold by William Mills & Son of New York circa 1920. Notice the tiny tip-top guide on the tip section which was designed to accommodate a fine silk line. The second tip, which is four inches short, has been modified with a modern Perfection guide to allow for casting of contemporary tapered, synthetic lines. This graceful rod is adorned with full intermediate red wraps, classic nickel-silver Leonard ferrules (1875 and 1878 patent dates), and a wood reel seat. The rod was discovered in its original brass-capped case and bag with the factory tag still attached. The original owners name is inked on the tag.

UNITED STATES PATENT OFFICE.

HIRAM L. LEONARD, OF BANGOR, MAINE.

IMPROVEMENT IN FISHING-RODS.

Specification forming part of Letters Patent No. **169,181**, dated October 26, 1875; application filed August 30, 1875.

To all whom it may concern:

Be it known that I, HIRAM L. LEONARD, of Bangor, in the county of Penobscot and State of Maine, have invented certain new and useful Improvements in Ferrules for Fishing-Rods; and I do hereby declare that the following is a full, clear, and exact description thereof, that will enable others skilled in the art to which it appertains to make and use the same, reference being had to the accompanying drawings forming a part of this specification, in which—

Figure 1 shows a section of my invention; Fig. 2, a modification of same.

Same letters show like parts.

My invention relates to the ferrules used to connect the parts of jointed fishing-rods, and is intended to prevent the access of water to the wooden portion of the rod. It is particularly applicable to rods made from segments of bamboo, united by glue, and known as "split-bamboo" rods. The outer surface of these rods is protected and rendered waterproof by varnish; but the ends, as heretofore constructed, have been unprotected. From the nature of their construction they are peculiarly liable to damage from moisture, which attacks and softens the glue which unites the parts, and eventually ruins the rod.

Reference to the accompanying drawing will assist in explaining my device. At *a* is shown one portion of a rod—for instance, the butt, having thereon the socket-ferrule *b* of the joint. This ferrule *b*, as constructed in my improved joint, may be termed an imperforate socket-ferrule, being so made that no water can penetrate through it to the wood of the rod. When the joint is made with a dowel and dowel-pin the ferrule *b* is provided with an imperforate socket, *d*, shaped to correspond to and receive the dowel-pin, and so fitted within the ferrule *b* as to prevent any access of water through or between the parts. Another form of construction is used when the joint is made without the dowel and pin, and this modification is shown in Fig. 2, the imperforate socket-ferrule being shown at *b'*, and being provided with a stop, *c'*, covering the end of the wooden portion of the rod. The next piece of the rod is also provided with an imperforate cap-ferrule, *e*, covering the end of the rod, and inclosing it and the dowel-pin in an impervious casing. The shoulders, formed by the dowel-pin and end of the rod, are stopped by an annular ring, *f*, so that no water can penetrate, and the end of the dowel-pin itself is covered by a cap, *p*. In the modification, Fig. 2, where no dowel-pin is used the end of the rod-joint is covered and made water-tight by a cap, *f'*, covering it, making its ferrule *e'* an impervious cap-ferrule.

For the purposes of illustration I have described the ferrules forming the first joint of the rod, but, as will be readily seen, my invention will apply equally to all the joints.

What I claim as my invention, and desire to secure by Letters Patent, is—

A joint for bamboo or other fishing-rods, consisting essentially of an imperforate cap-ferrule, in combination with a correspondingly-shaped and imperforate socket-ferrule, substantially as and for the purposes set forth.

In testimony that I claim the foregoing, I have hereunto set my hand this 27th day of August, 1875.

HIRAM L. LEONARD.

Witnesses:
J. P. BASS,
WM. FRANKLIN SEAVEY.

The original text in the application for patent No. 169,181 (granted October 26. 1875). Despite the requisite legalese, Leonard's genius and logic are clearly evident.

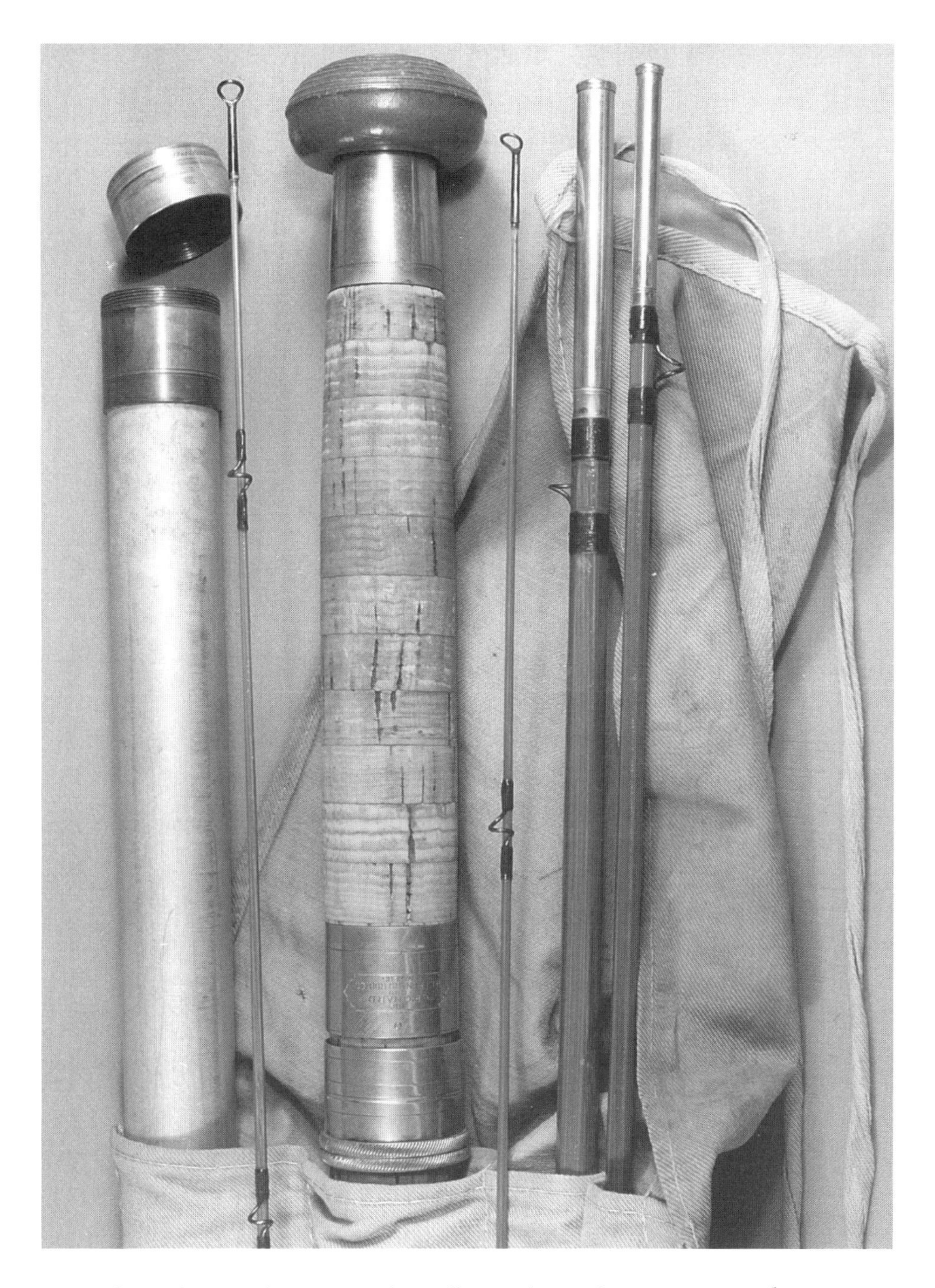

H.L. Leonard 13 foot salmon (grilse) fly rod made in 1930. This massive four piece, 15 7/8 oz. rod includes two tips enclosed in a narrow aluminum tip-tube with a screw-on brass cap. The tip-tube, two mid, and butt sections fit into the original heavy canvas bag shown here. The reel seat is constructed of cork and fine nickel-silver sliding bands for reel retention. Upon close inspection, the fine diameter of the tips can be seen, providing a clue to the rod's utility in light salmon (grilse) angling.

Joint for Fishing-Rod.

No. 207,665. Patented Sept. 3, 1878.

Fig. 2.

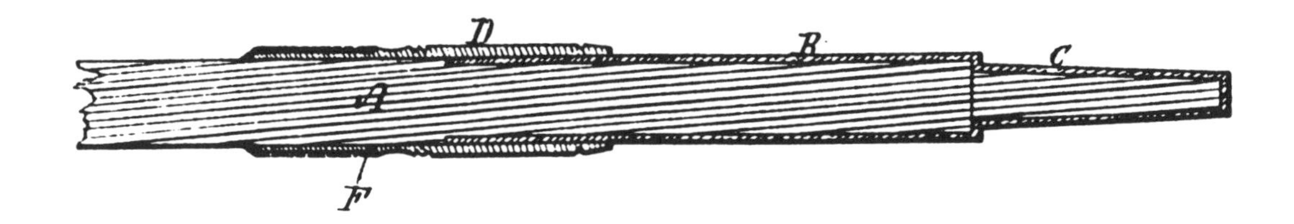

The 1878 Leonard patent drawing is shown here. An improvement to the previous patent can best be explained in the inventor's own words . . . *This invention relates to means for strengthening the joints of fishing rods, or the pieces composing the various lengths of the rod, at the point of junction with the ferrules; and consists in the employment of a* ***split tube*** *extending from the outer end of the ferrule and inclosing the said piece, the purpose of the invention being to strengthen what has heretofore been considered the weakest part of the rod without interfering with its elasticity.* Leonard split (serrated) an extension of the ferrule (part **F** figure **1**) by sawing at several points a saw-kerf (parts **a** figure **1**) thus forming a more flexible transition at the point where the ferrule and bamboo met. To protect the area from moisture, he wound silk over the split extension and thoroughly varnished the outside. The diameter of the split extension was reduced so that it would be flush with the rest of the ferrule (part **D** figure **2)** when the bulk of the silk was added after installation.

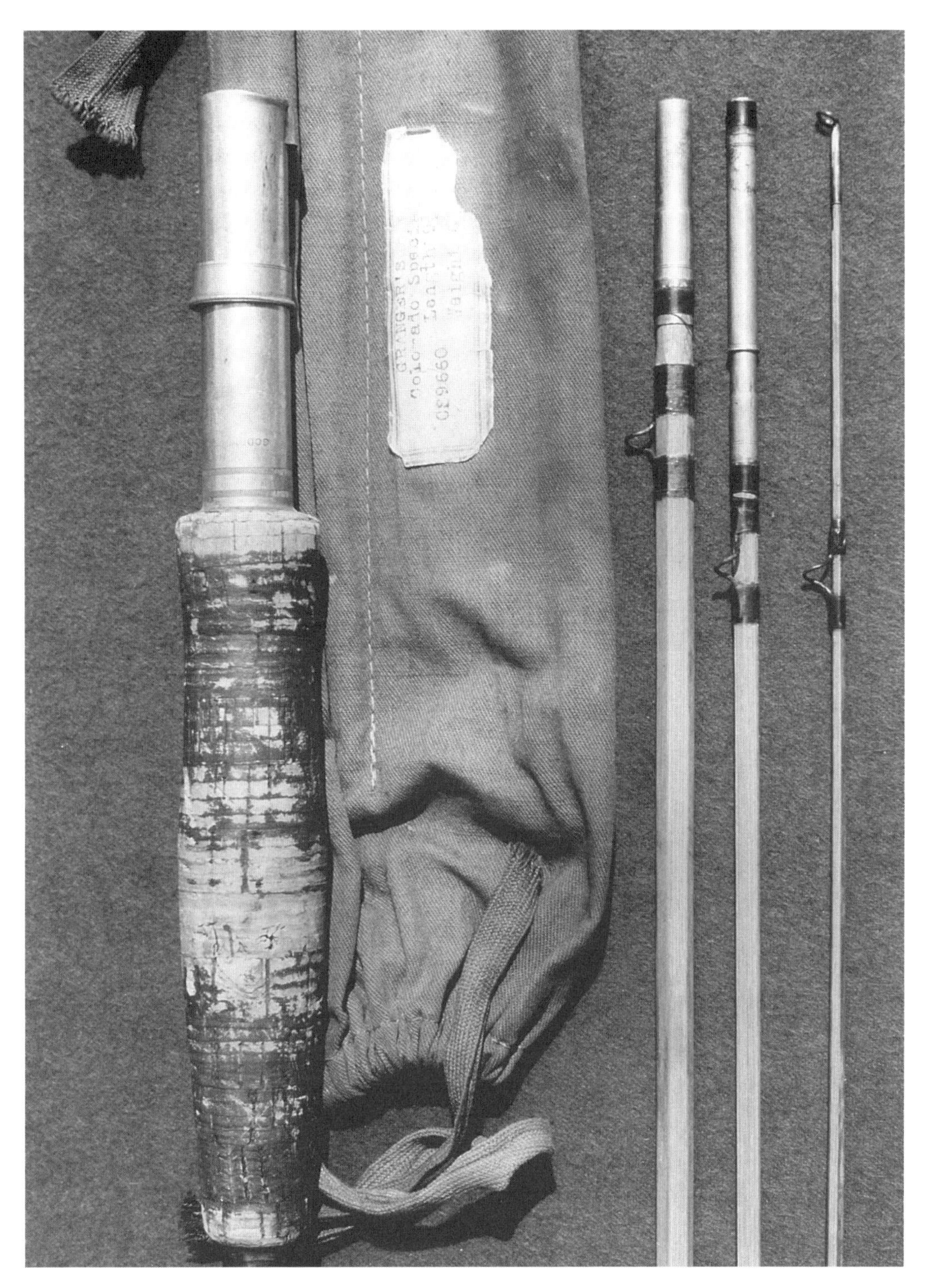

Early three piece Goodwin Granger *Colorado Special* (9 1/2') bamboo fly rod built circa 1929 in Denver, Colorado. Features include the familiar Granger nickel-silver slide band reel seat and light cane finish. This example suffers from several maladies, the most noticeable being a ferrule detached from the cane at the mid-joint.

T. H. CHUBB.
Reel Fastener for Fishing Rods.

No. 235,511. **Patented Dec. 14, 1880.**

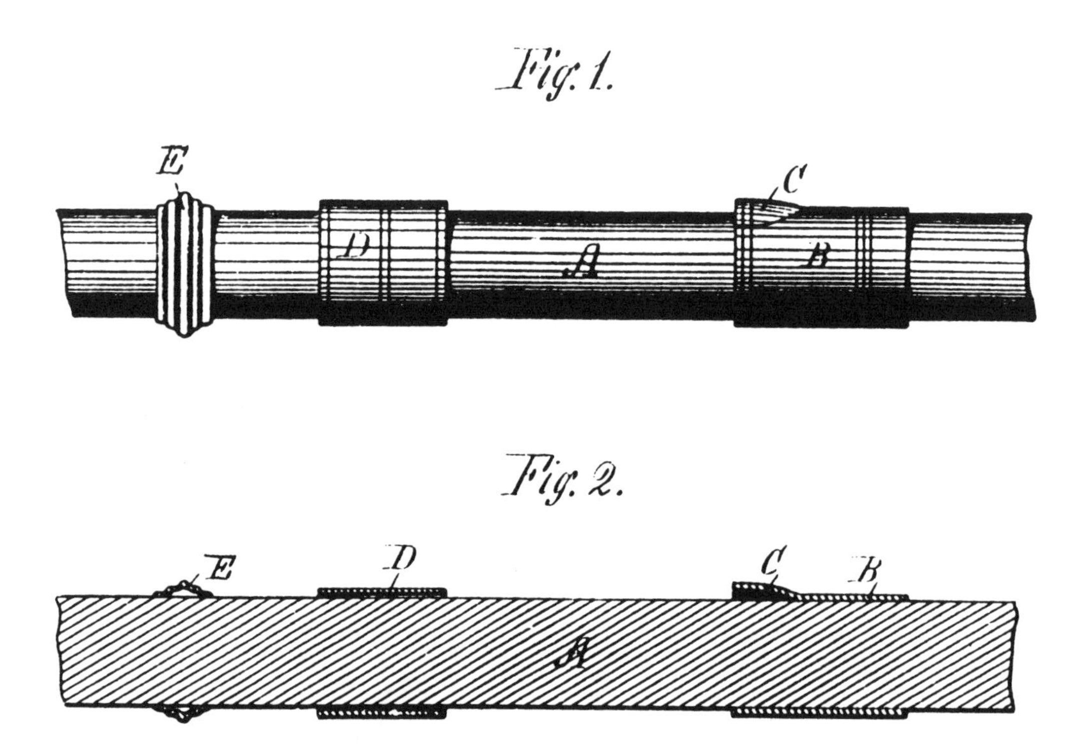

Thomas Chubb is credited with having invented the first slide band reel seat, the forerunner of many quality fly rod reel seats, including the Goodwin Granger design shown on the previous page. The 1880 Chubb patent is pictured above. It had been common practice, prior to Chubb's invention, to cut a recess in the surface of the butt material as a receiver of the reel foot — thus the reel would be prevented from turning or shifting. In Chubb's own words . . . *I dispense with the recess . . . and to prevent turning or shifting of the reel upon the rod I employ a short tube or sleeve (**B**) to encompass the butt, and strike up in or add to the upper end of such sleeve a swell or inclosure (**C**) which is adapted to receive the lower end of the reel-plate (foot) and confine it closely to the surface of the butt. Above the sleeve (**B**) I employ a loose ring (**D**) and a stop-ring (**E**).*

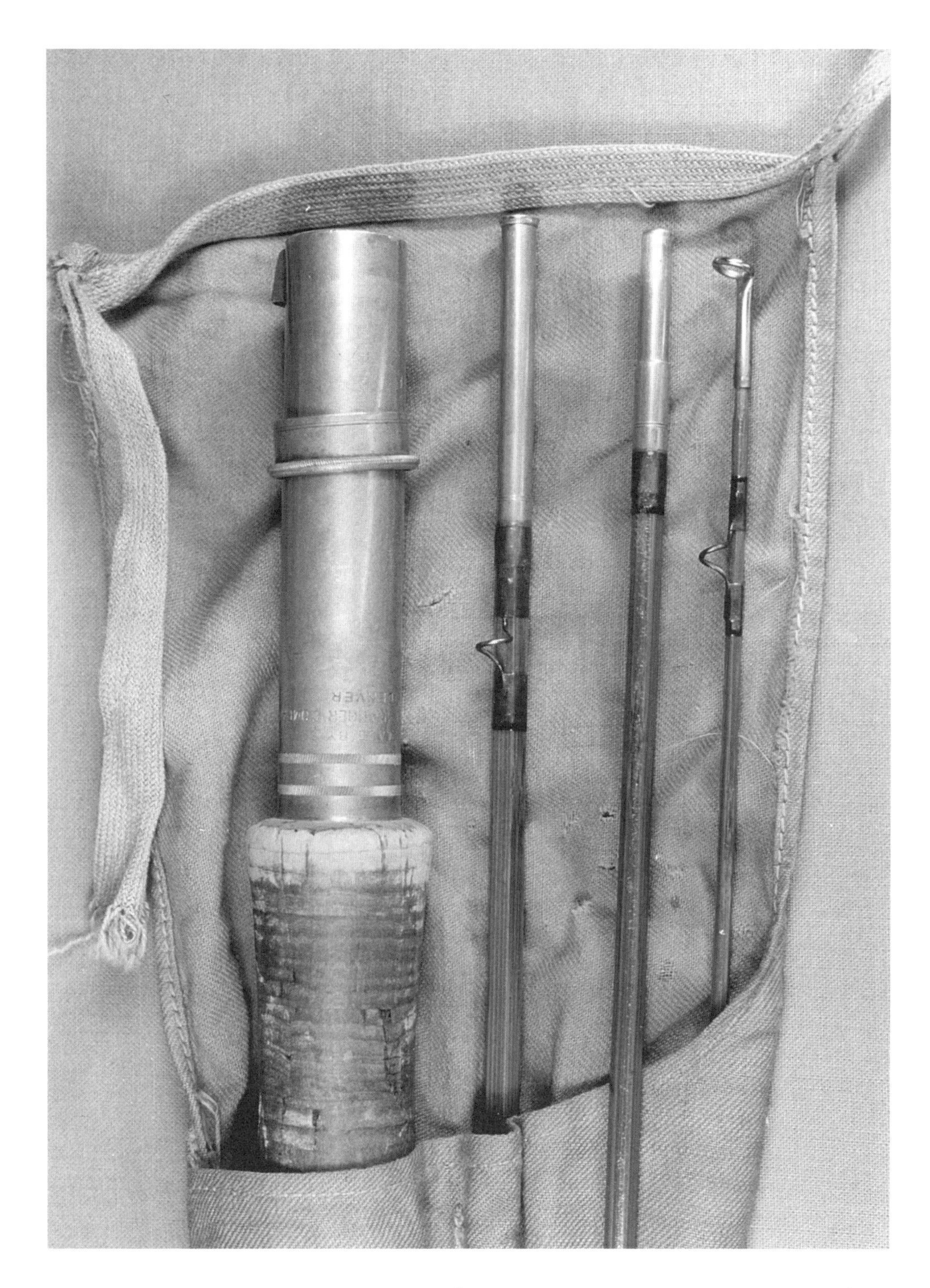

Later Goodwin Granger *Champion*, a light 9 foot trout model (3 piece with 2 tips). Wraps are red with black accents. This is an exceptionally good split bamboo rod for modern use that will not cost an arm and a leg! The varnish has some rough spots, yet it is still sound and serviceable. The tip-top guide needs to be re-set.

Wright & McGill *Granger Special* (3 piece with 2 tips) featuring the patented (1938) screw up-locking reel seat. This is a much sought-after 8 1/2 foot bamboo trout fly rod complete with original bag, case, and inter-changeable heavy and light tips.

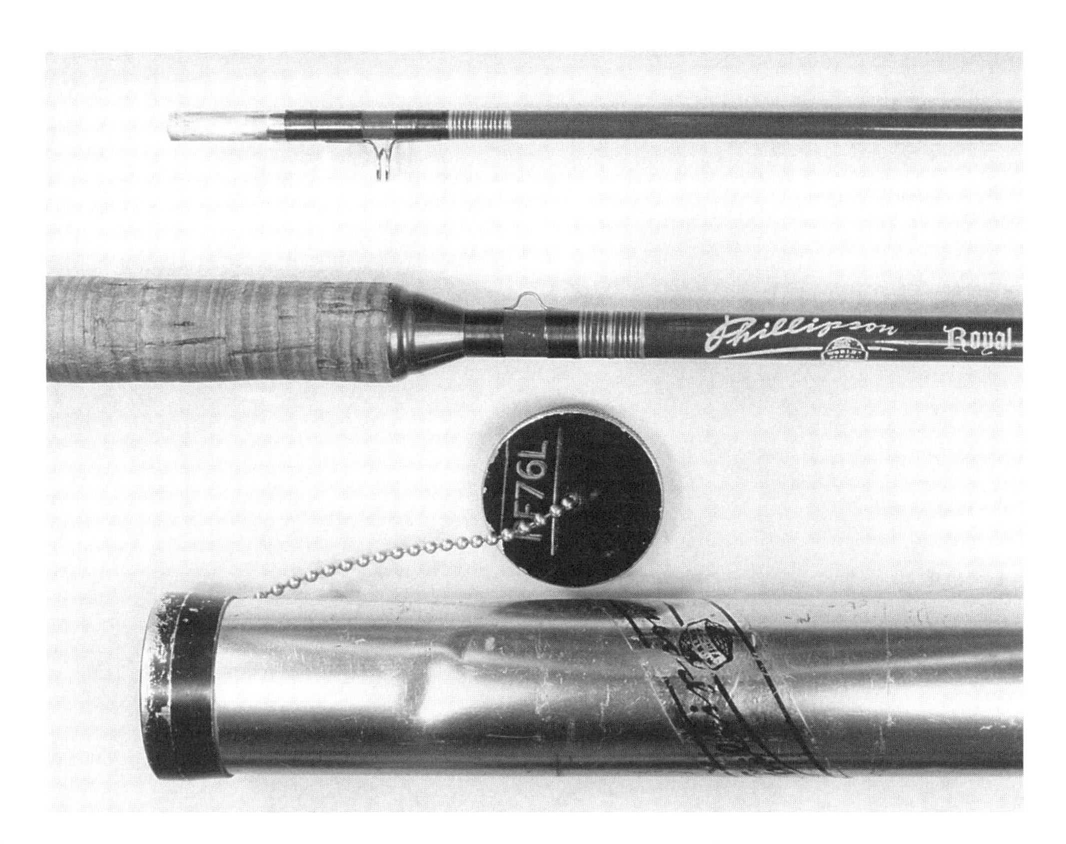

Phillipson Rod Company of Colorado made some of the best fiberglass fly rods of the 1960 to 1970 era. This 7 1/2′ Phillipson *Royal* is no exception.

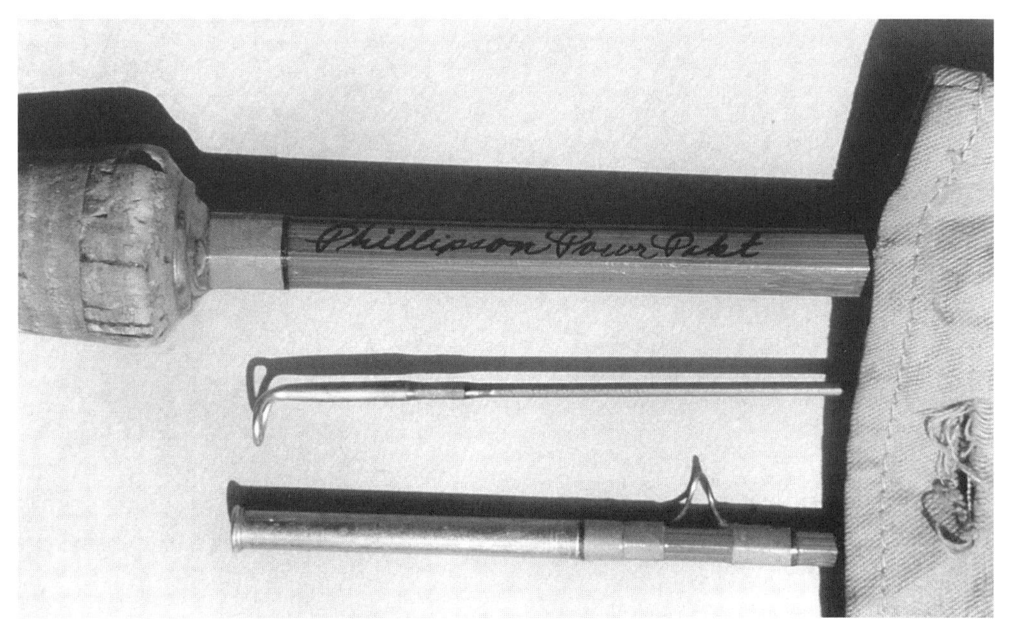

Bill Phillipson *Power-Pakt,* a fast action bamboo fly rod from the 1950s. Guide wraps are yellow with black accents. This is an early varnished Phillipson.

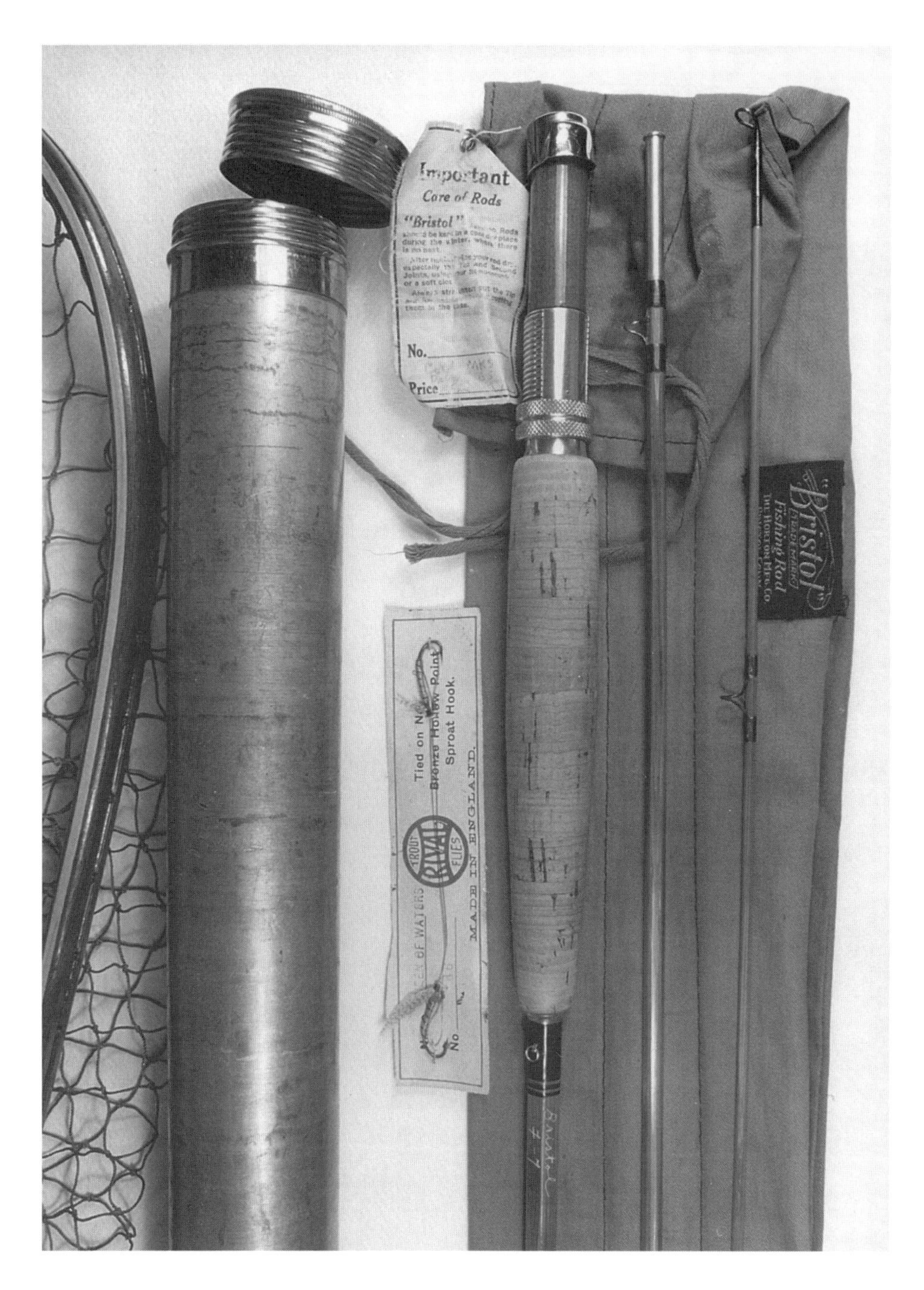

A lovely Bristol Model F-7 bamboo fly rod made by Edwards and marketed by the Horton Manufacturing Co. This 9 foot, three-piece trout rod would be graded in excellent condition, <u>but for</u> a broken extra tip (not shown). Although the F-7 reel seat hardware is chrome plated, it is complemented by a fine walnut insert. Ferrules are quality nickel-silver. The original bag with "Care of Rods" tag is displayed here.

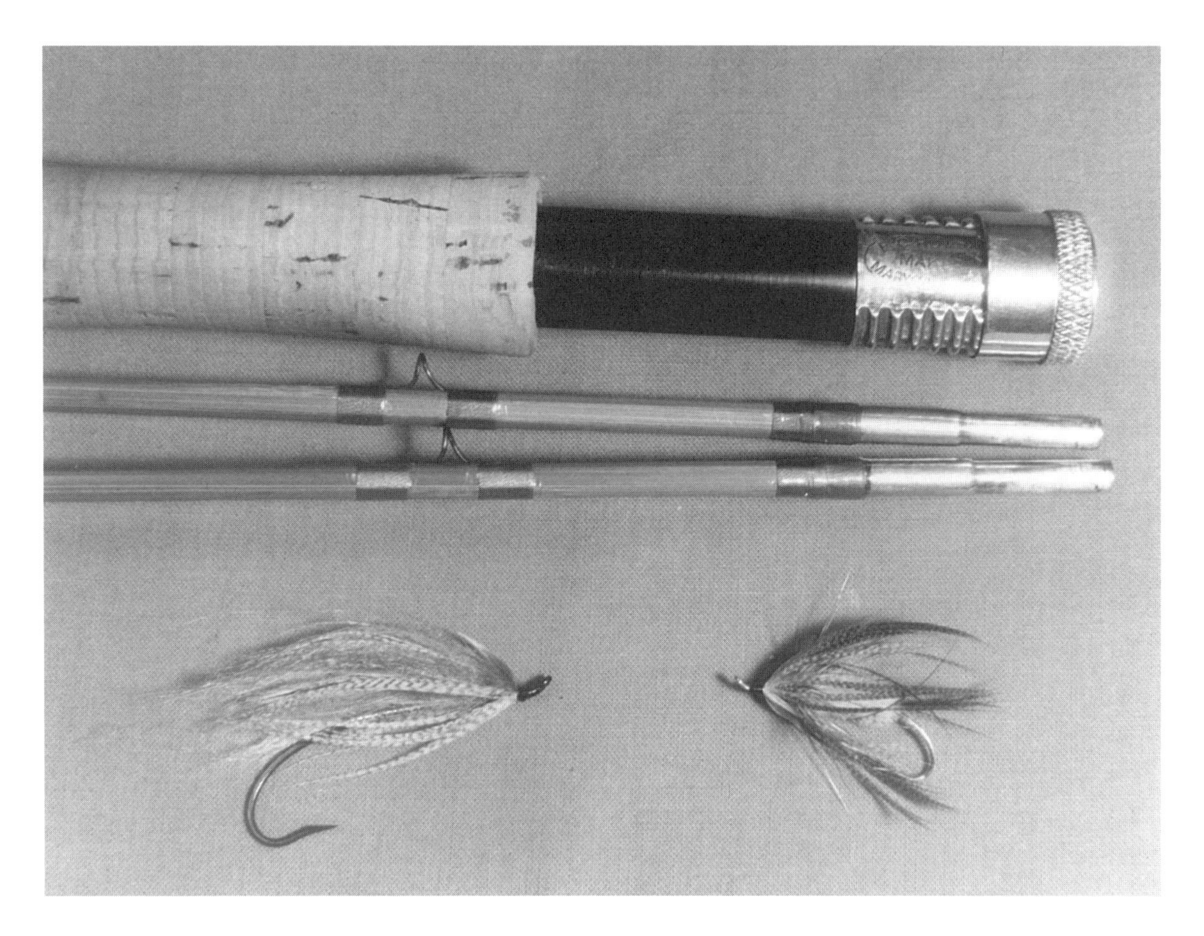

7 1/2' E.C. Powell trout fly rod (2 piece, 2 tip) made in Marysville, California circa 1949. Powell was well known for his long, powerful steelhead fly rods designed to be very light as a result of a unique bamboo and wood core construction process which is now recognized as the famous patent #1,932,986 (found inked on the shaft of many Powell rods). The rational, as stated by Edwin Powell himself is as follows . . . *I have found that bamboo, with few exceptions, grows so that the outside portion is very dense with fibres, but that these fibres gradually lessen in density until the structure becomes almost entirely pith. Occasionally a cane is found within a thin rind of very dense fibres that breaks off suddenly into pith. This latter form of growth gives the desired results as to a combination of strength and great lightness, but such canes are so few that they cannot be depended on as a source of supply for the manufacturing of fishing rods. I have therefore reconstructed the bamboo so that I obtain artificially, and in any quantity, rods having a combination of strength and lightness substantially equivalent to that found in the last mentioned type of bamboo cane* **(See drawing on next page)** . . . *I make a wooden core (sugar pine) of as many segments (**part 2**) as there are strips (**part 1**) each such segment being thus of triangular cross section as shown. Each bamboo strip is glued to the outer face of the corresponding core segment throughout its length before the segments are assembled.*

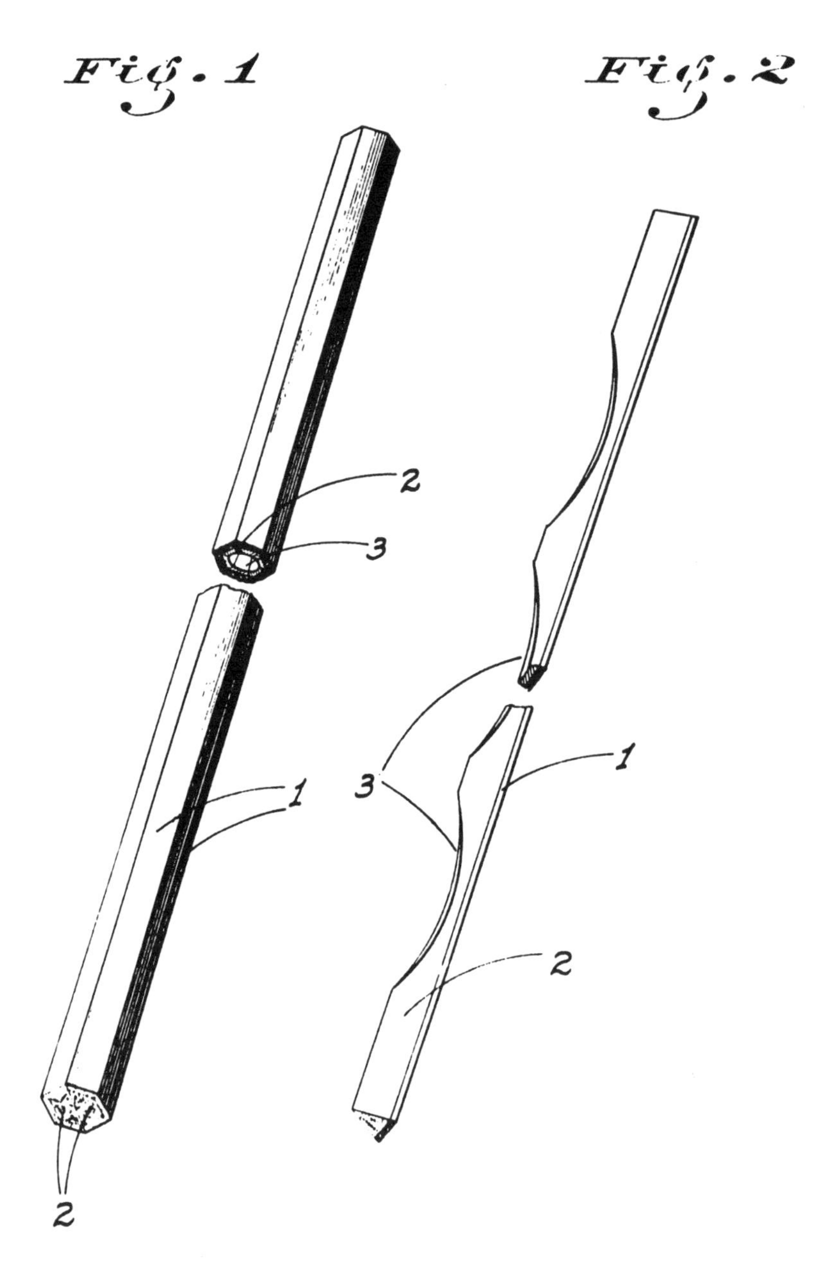

The E.C. Powell patent of October 31, 1933. In the actual construction of the rod, the bamboo strips (**part 1**) were rough-cut to size after being split from the bamboo culm. The strips were then glued onto rectangular slabs of wood. After drying, the glued-up unit was further cut to the proper sixty-degree triangular shape necessary to make the finished hexagonal rod section. At this point, the wood-core portion of the segment was gouged out at intervals as shown in **part 3**. So as not to weaken the rod, the core segments were <u>not</u> gouged out (left solid) at the ferrules. Finally, the various segmental units were assembled and secured together by glue applied along the side faces of the core segments and strips.

F.E. Thomas bamboo salmon fly rod from Bangor, Maine. Of special note for identification purposes is a reel seat patented June 24, 1913 (the patent date appears on the opposite side of the seat shown). This is an adjustable reel holding mechanism whereby springs on the securing band engage two ratchet-toothed ridges along the sleeve of the seat. The Thomas signature wraps can also be seen at the base of the blued ferrules.

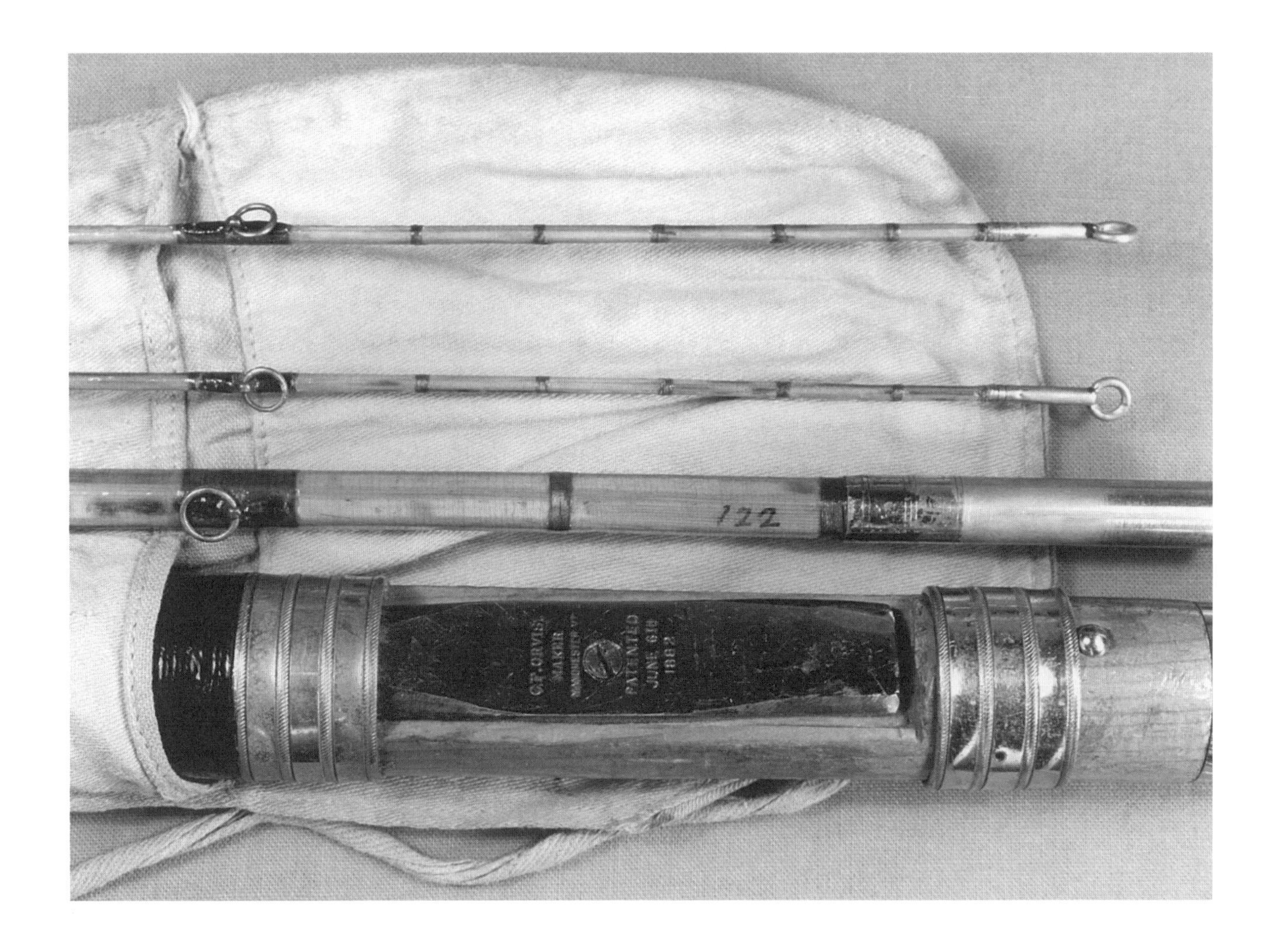

Three piece Charles F. Orvis antique Calcutta bamboo fly rod — 11 feet long with two full length tips. The venerable Orvis 1882 patented reel seat is pictured close-up. The nice thing about this particular early Orvis is the fact that its original flip-ring guides and wraps are intact and in good repair. Many historic 1880 to 1890 era American made fly rods have long since been refinished, the flip-ring guides having been replaced with snake guides. Notice that one of the fixed reel bands, which was originally pinned to the wood handle, has been converted to a sliding band (with the small screw added as a stopper). This is the only modification detracting from the rod's excellent condition. The black, cord-whipped grip was a standard Orvis feature — an all sumac wood handpiece was also available according to a circa 1889 catalog.

H. EGGLESTON.

REEL SEAT FOR FISHING RODS.

No. 258,902. Patented June 6, 1882.

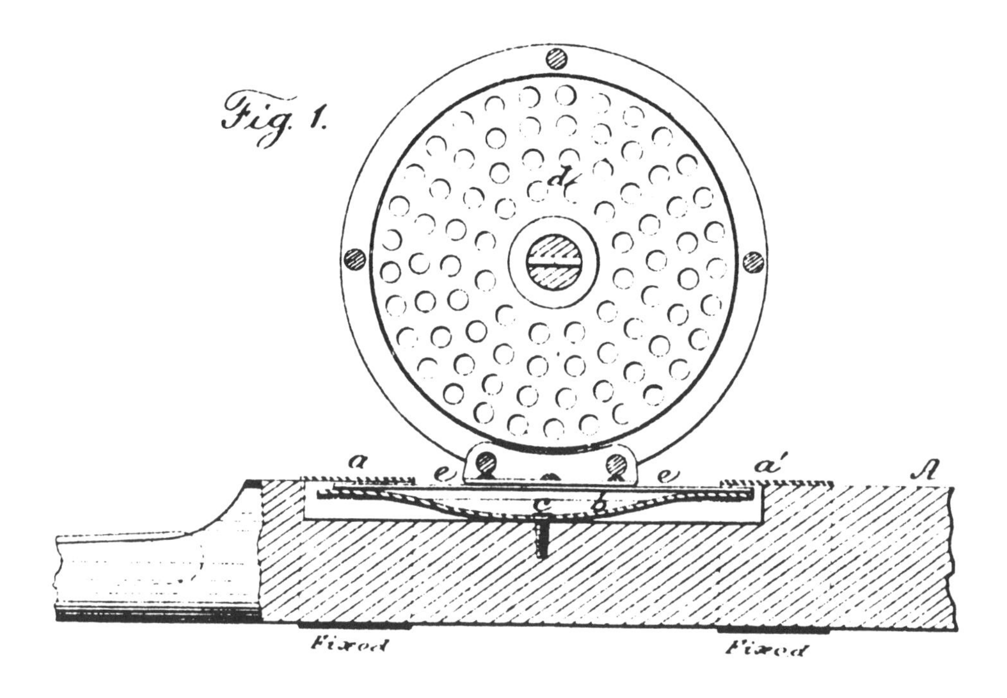

The Hiram Eggleston invention called a "spring loaded reel seat" was assigned to Charles Orvis and patented June 6, 1882. The motivation of the inventor is explained in the patent application as follows . . . *the usual fastening for the reel is a fixed and a sliding band on the butt of the rod adapted to receive and fasten the ends of the seat plate of the reel* (reel foot) *in the seat of the butt* . . . (however) *the sliding band is liable to become loose, to fail in giving a firm clamping hold . . . the object of my improvement is to provide a simple and safe fastening for the reel, while allowing its being readily fastened to and removed from the rod.* Eggleston's reel seat was equipped with two fixed bands (**a**) positioned on both ends of a spring-seat plate (**b**) which is directly recessed into a longitudinal excavation in the butt material and secured by a center screw (**c**). The ends of the spring plate curve outward from the recess and extend under the fixed rings. The reel was fastened by placing the reel foot one end at a time onto the spring plate while pushing down.

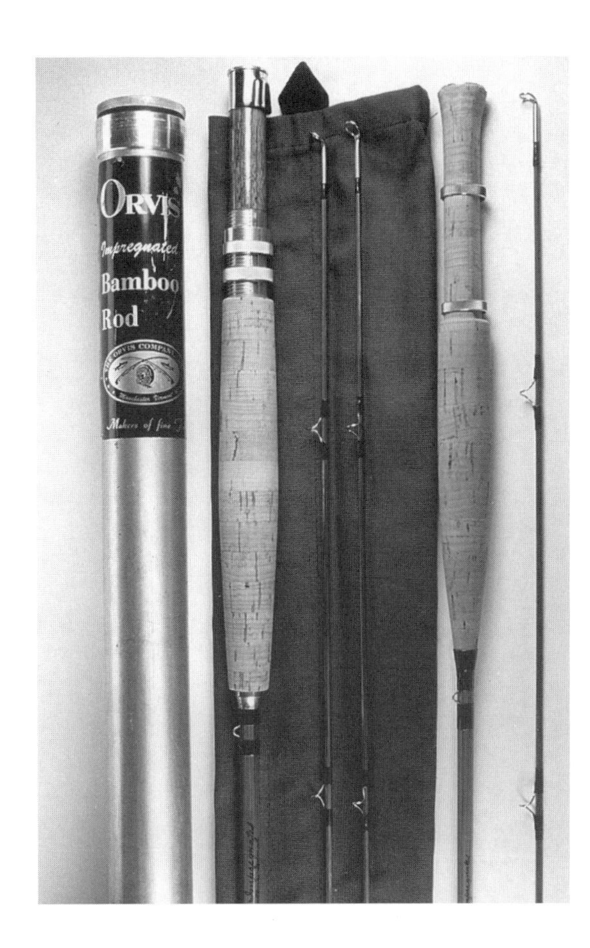

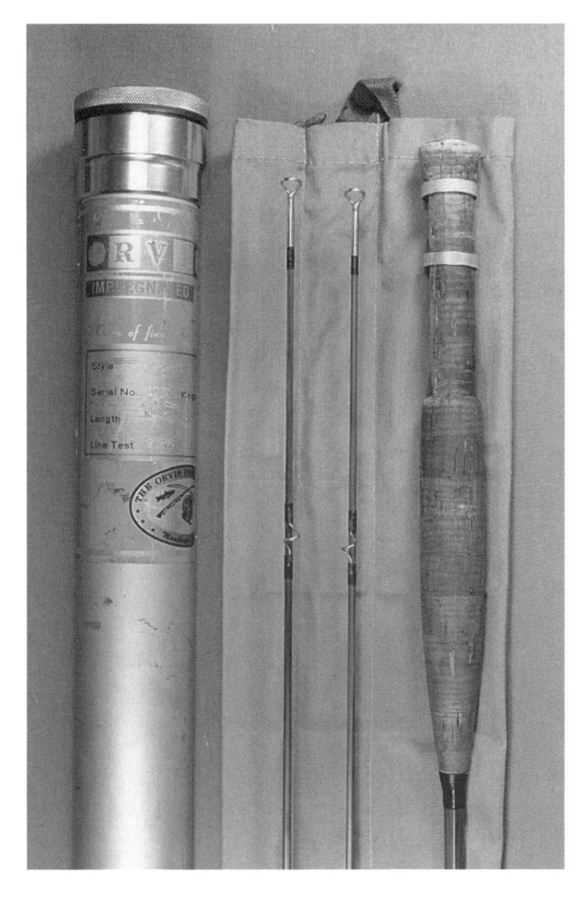

Orvis trout fly rods circa 1960-1970. (**Left to right**) The 8 1/2 foot *Battenkill Limestone Special* is a two-piece, two tip rod with a walnut insert affixed to the standard chrome Orvis screw-locking reel seat. The next rod is a 6 1/2 foot *Madison Flea* model which was originally equipped with only one tip. It features a traditional, light cork sliding band reel seat. On the far right is a 6 1/2 foot *Superfine*. All rods are Bakelite impregnated. The process of impregnating bamboo with liquid resin (Bakelite) was invented in 1946 by Wes Jordan, head rod designer for The Orvis Company of Manchester, Vermont. The patent (granted in 1950) was assigned to Orvis. The process described by Jordan indicates that the six triangular rod segments are prepared in the customary way when making split bamboo rods (split from the whole culm, node-sanded, and suitably milled). The six segments are then loosely banded together and dipped in a bath of special bakelite resin. Immediately after removal from the bath, the segments are tightly bound by machine and left to dry. The bound segments are subsequently cured in an oven, cleaned and the whole blank is then subjected to one final immersion process — first in water, and finally in a different bakelite solution for several days . . . *in such a manner as to effect thorough impregnation of the cells and fibers of the bamboo between the cemented joints.*

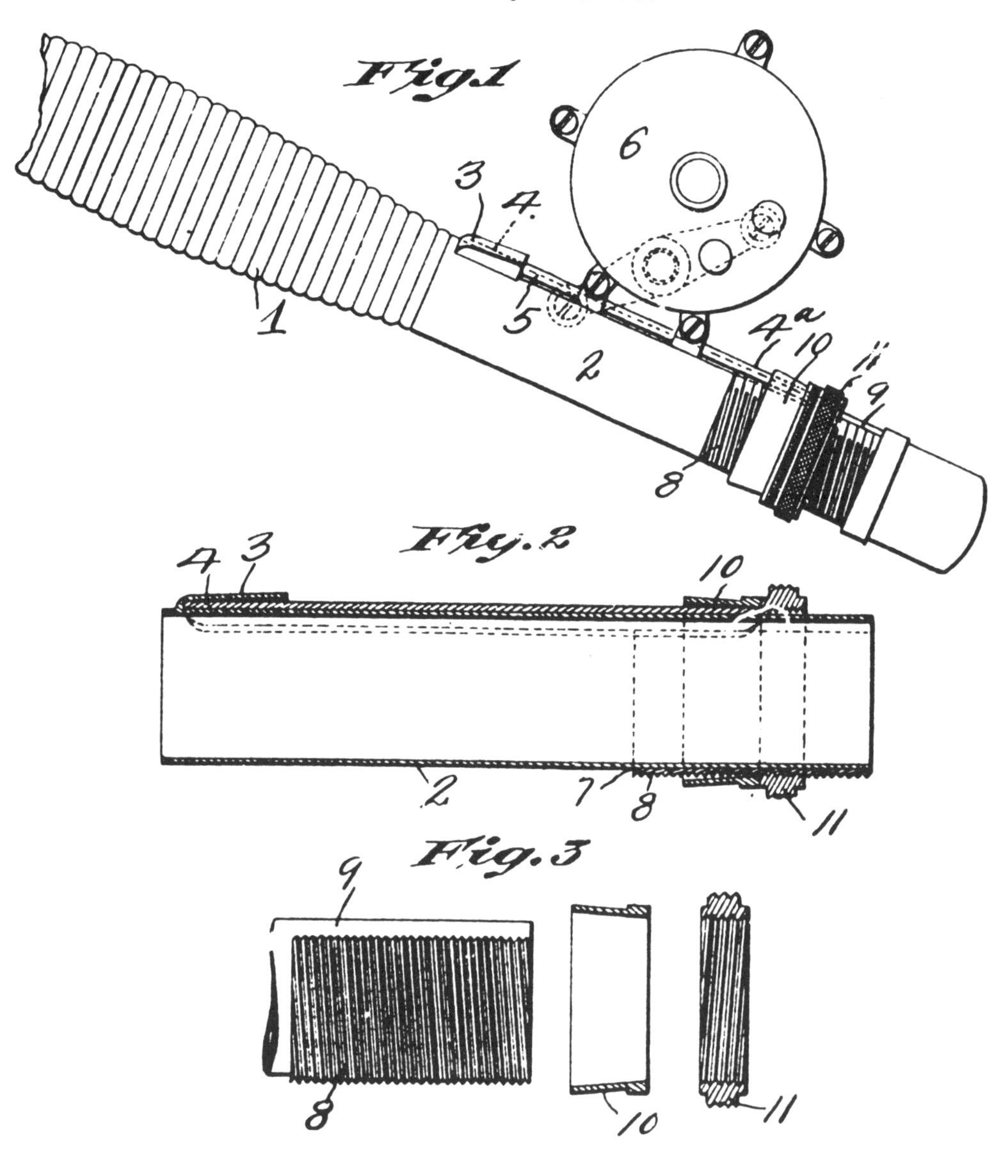

The patent drawing from Wesley Jordan's original version of the screw-lock reel seat. The patent was granted in 1927 and assigned to South Bend Bait Company of Indiana, where Jordan supervised rod making operations at that time. His intent as stated in the patent application was . . . *to provide a fishing reel plate* (foot) *jamming sleeve independent of a jam nut thereby insuring a positive holding of the plate* (foot) *and at the same time obviating friction, which is one of the common objections now experience where the sleeve and nut are formed integral.*

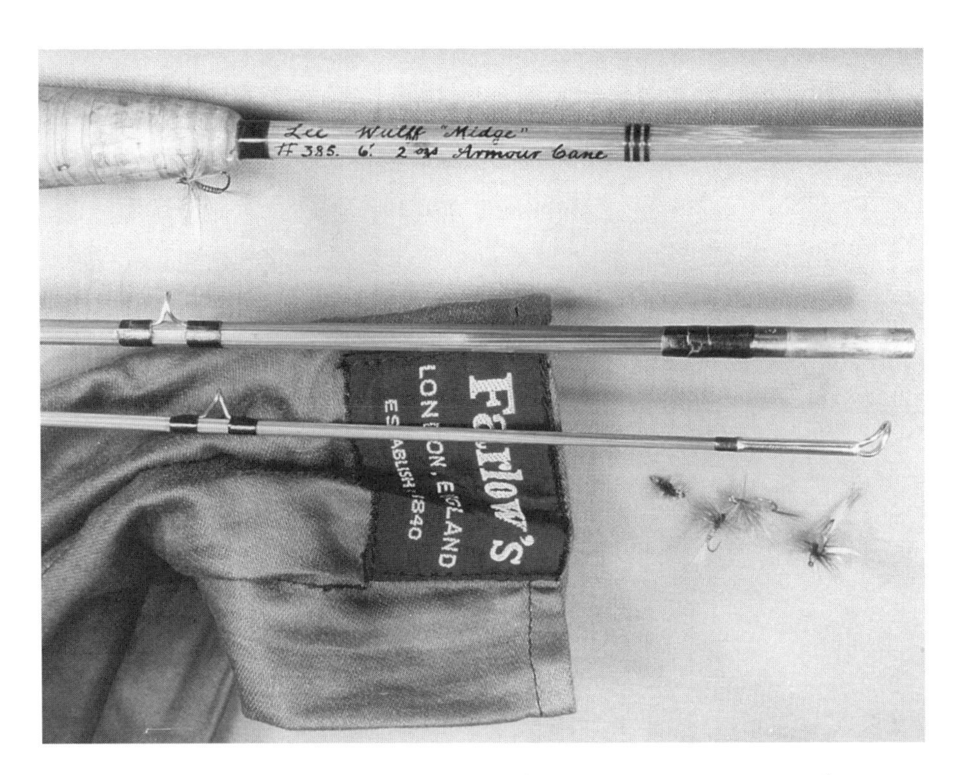

A Farlow *Lee Wulff Midge* sold by Norm Thompson. Many of the later Farlow bamboo rods (some made by Sharpe's of Aberdeen, Scotland) were bakelite impregnated as was this tiny six foot, two-piece trout model.

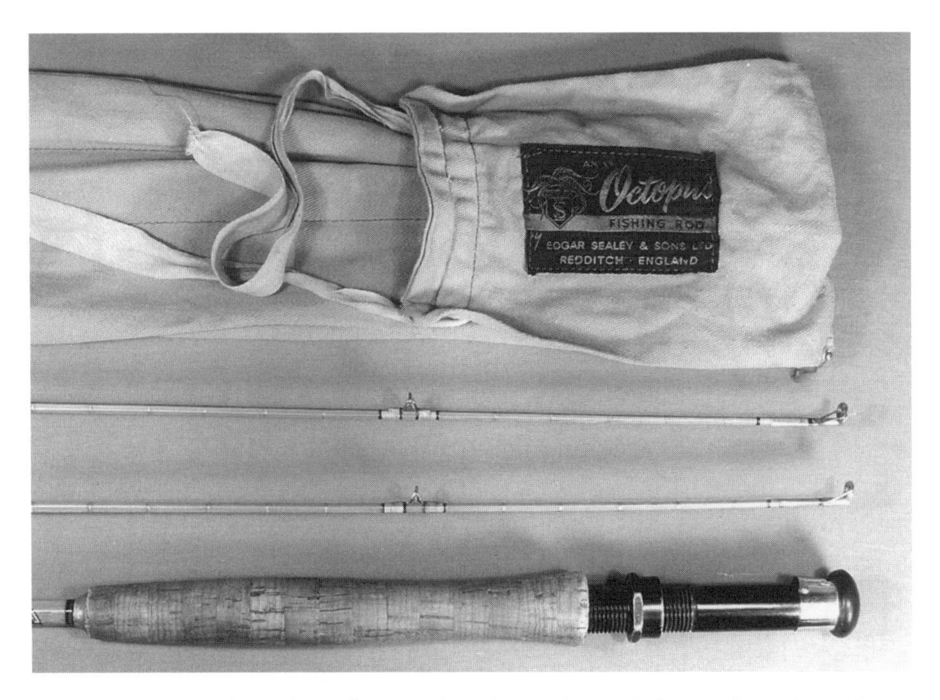

Edgar Sealey & Sons of Redditch, England marketed these familiar *Octopus* bamboo fly rods during the 1960s. They are sturdy and fit for modern use.

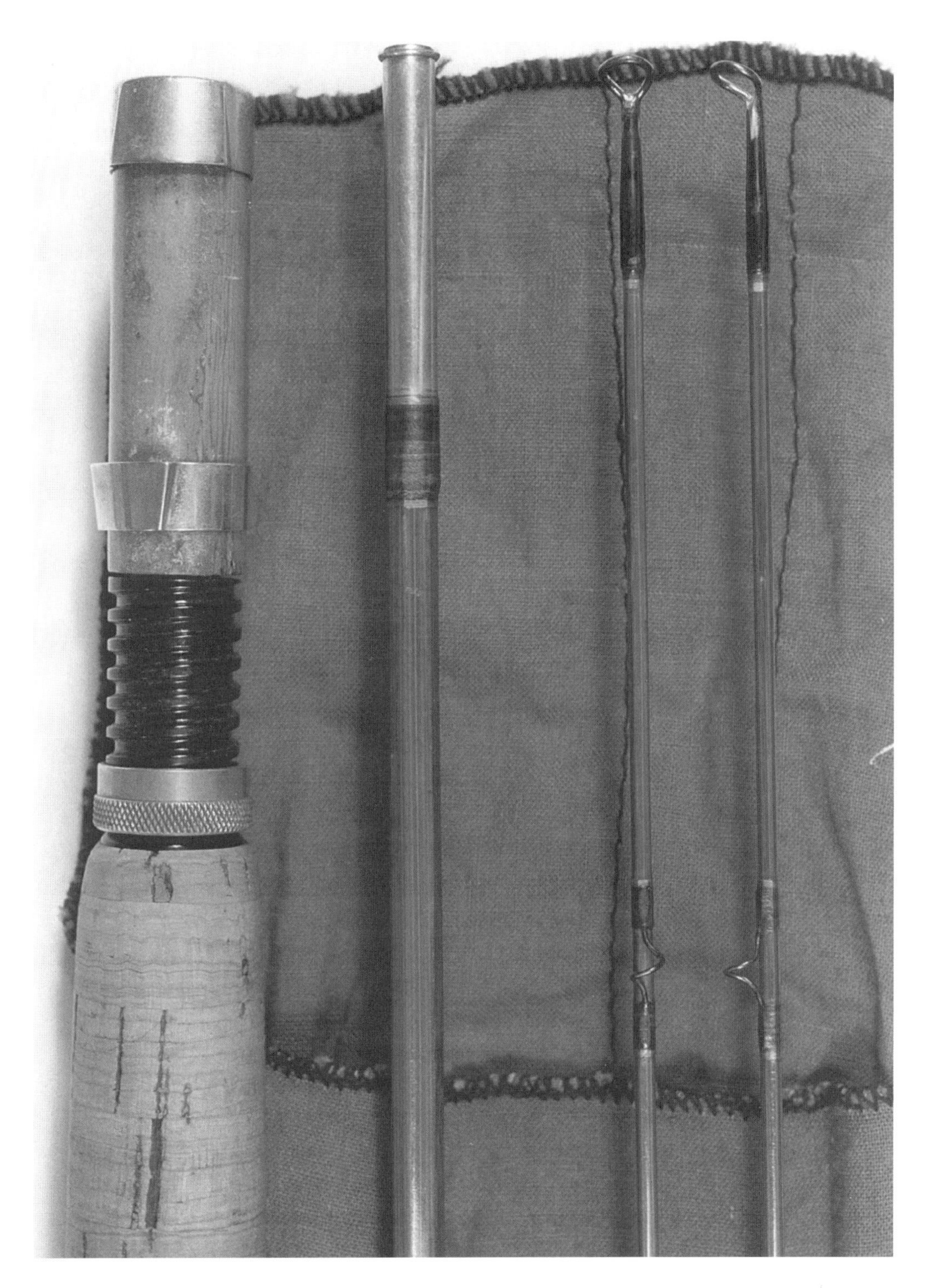

Heddon made this outstanding Model #1515 bamboo trout rod for The Folsom Arms Company. It is the equivalent of a high grade Heddon Model 35 *Peerless*, having nickel-silver hardware and a light wood reel seat insert. Rod exhibits delicate tips, and at 9 feet can accomplish long, smooth presentations.

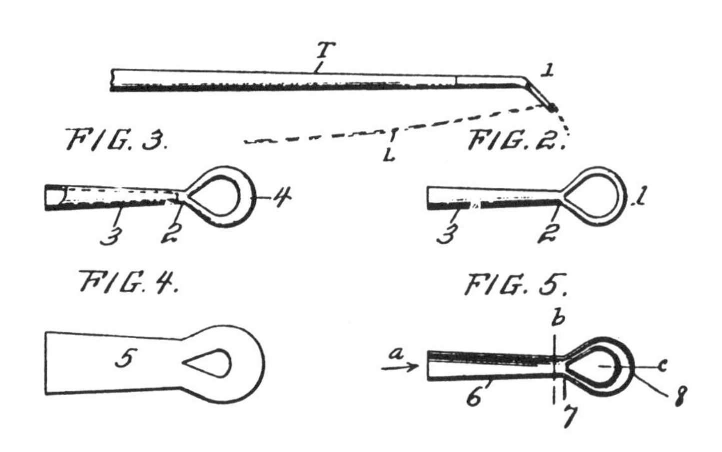

Patent shown above is known as the *Perfection* tip-top guide, now practically affixed to most fly rods. The object of the pear shape was to make it . . . *almost impossible for the line to catch around it.*

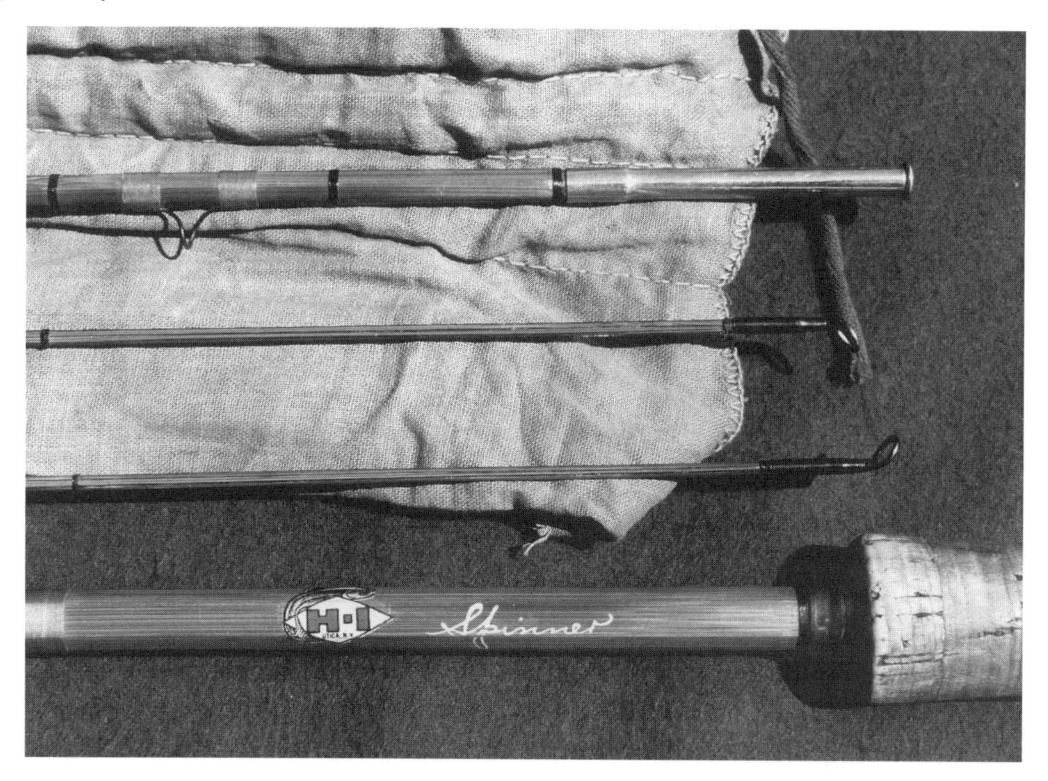

A Horrock - Ibbotson *Spinner* bamboo fly rod with its attractive decal intact.

Older rod with intermediate wraps is a 9 1/2 foot H & I *Catskill Model*, which was discovered in the original felt-covered wood form case (**far right**). Shown at mid-photo is the Horrocks - Ibbotson *Beaverkill*, an 8 1/2 foot bamboo trout rod found in the original bag with cloth label, missing a tip — but in very good condition. Must deduct some value for the missing tip.

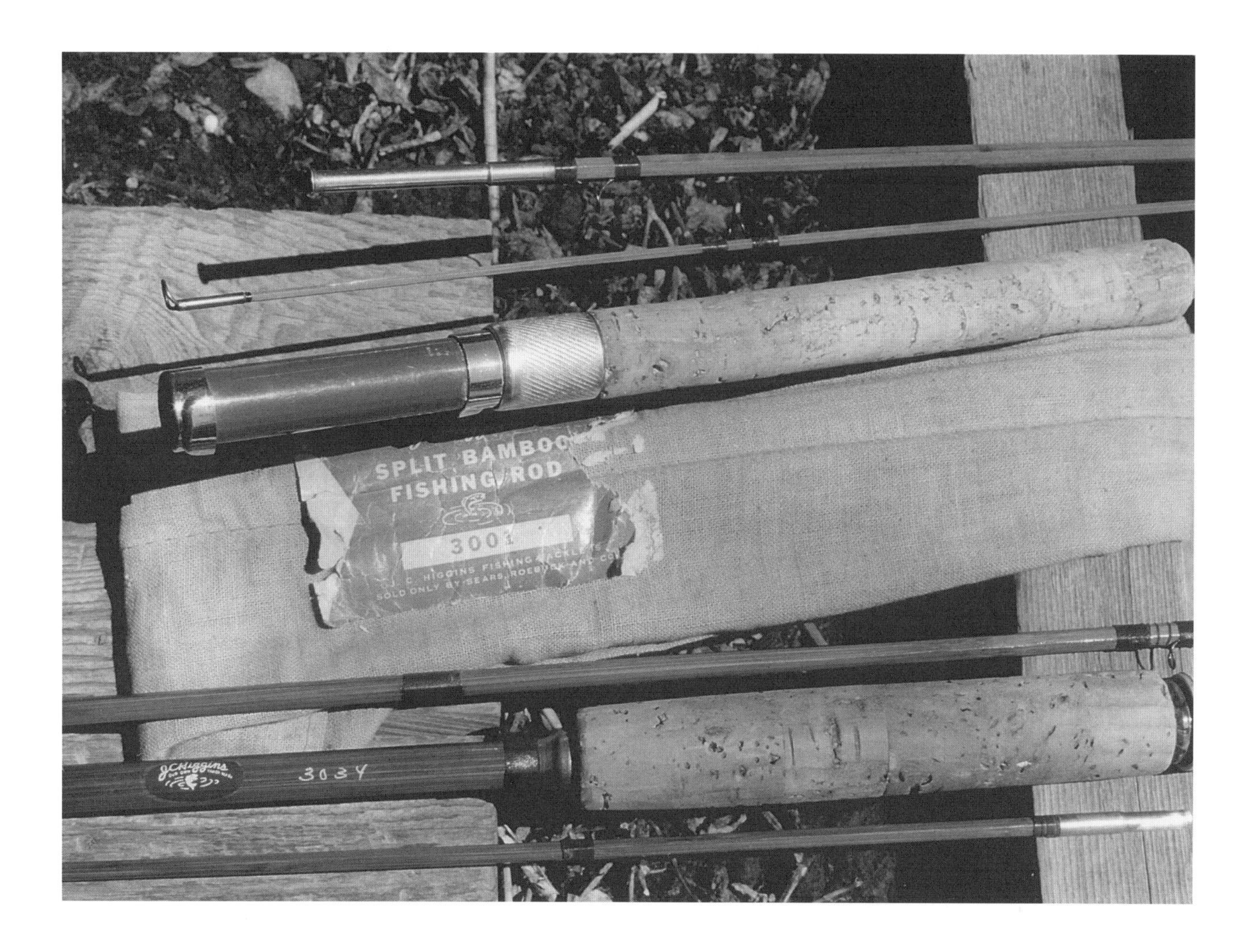

Pictured above are two good examples of private label bamboo fly rods made circa 1950. Both rods bear the *J. C. Higgins* label, a trade name for Sears. The rod at top is a Model 3001 and was produced by the Montague Rod & Reel Company for Sears. It is equipped with the same reel seat Montague utilized on their *Clipper* fly rods. The lower rod is a Model 3034 made by H & I. Private label rods are interesting to collect and most are reasonably priced. Difficulty in identification arises when a retailer had rods produced for them by several different manufacturers. Phillipson, Heddon, Edwards, and other top makers also produced rods under private label agreement with various retail and mail order companies — so take a close look.

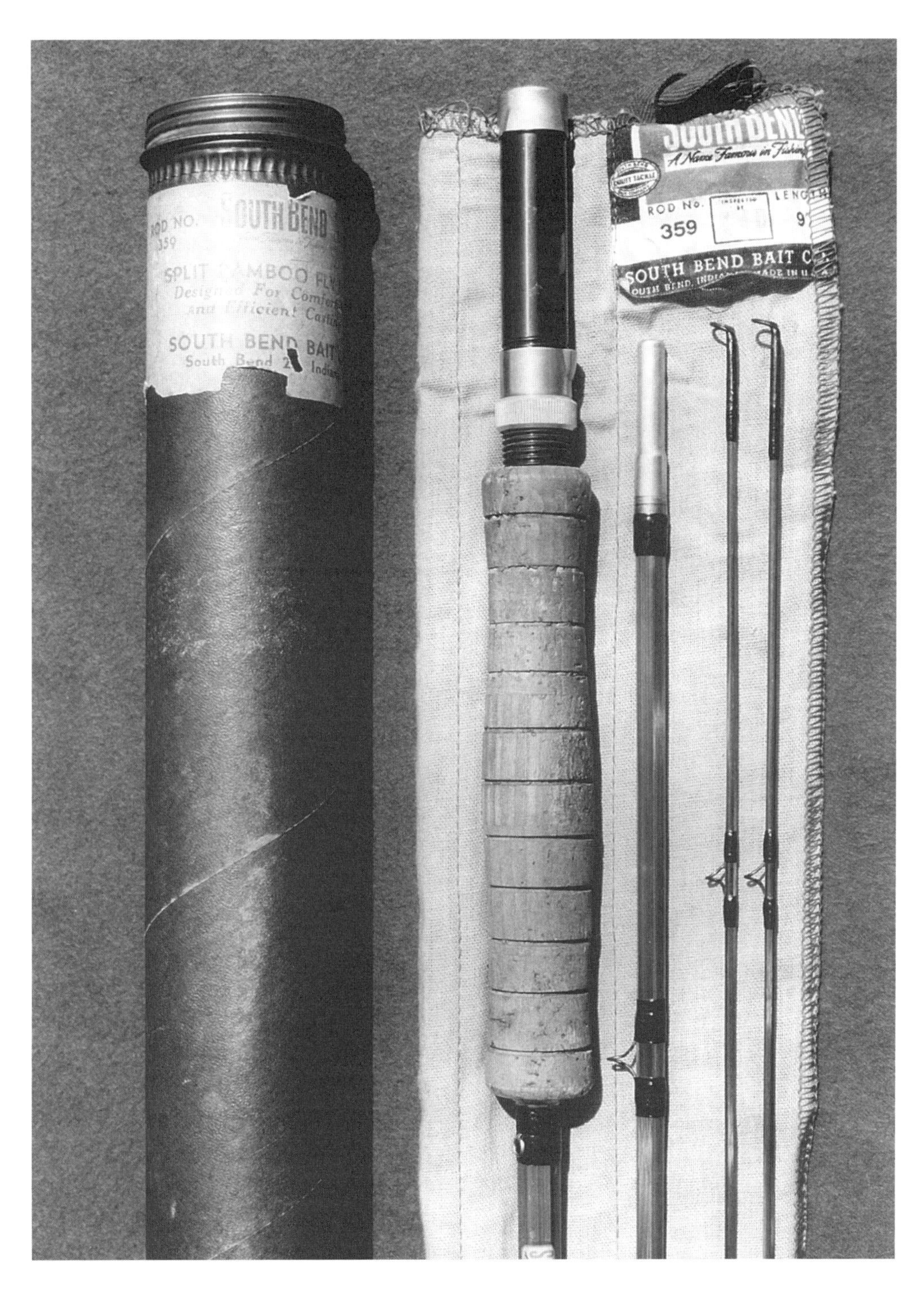

South Bend Model 359 "flamed" bamboo fly rod with aluminum ferrules is complete with two tips, original bag, and screw-capped, cardboard fiber tube. Many of these 9 footers were sold in the late 1940s and 50s. This model featured a recessed thumb rest that was sculpted into the cork grip.

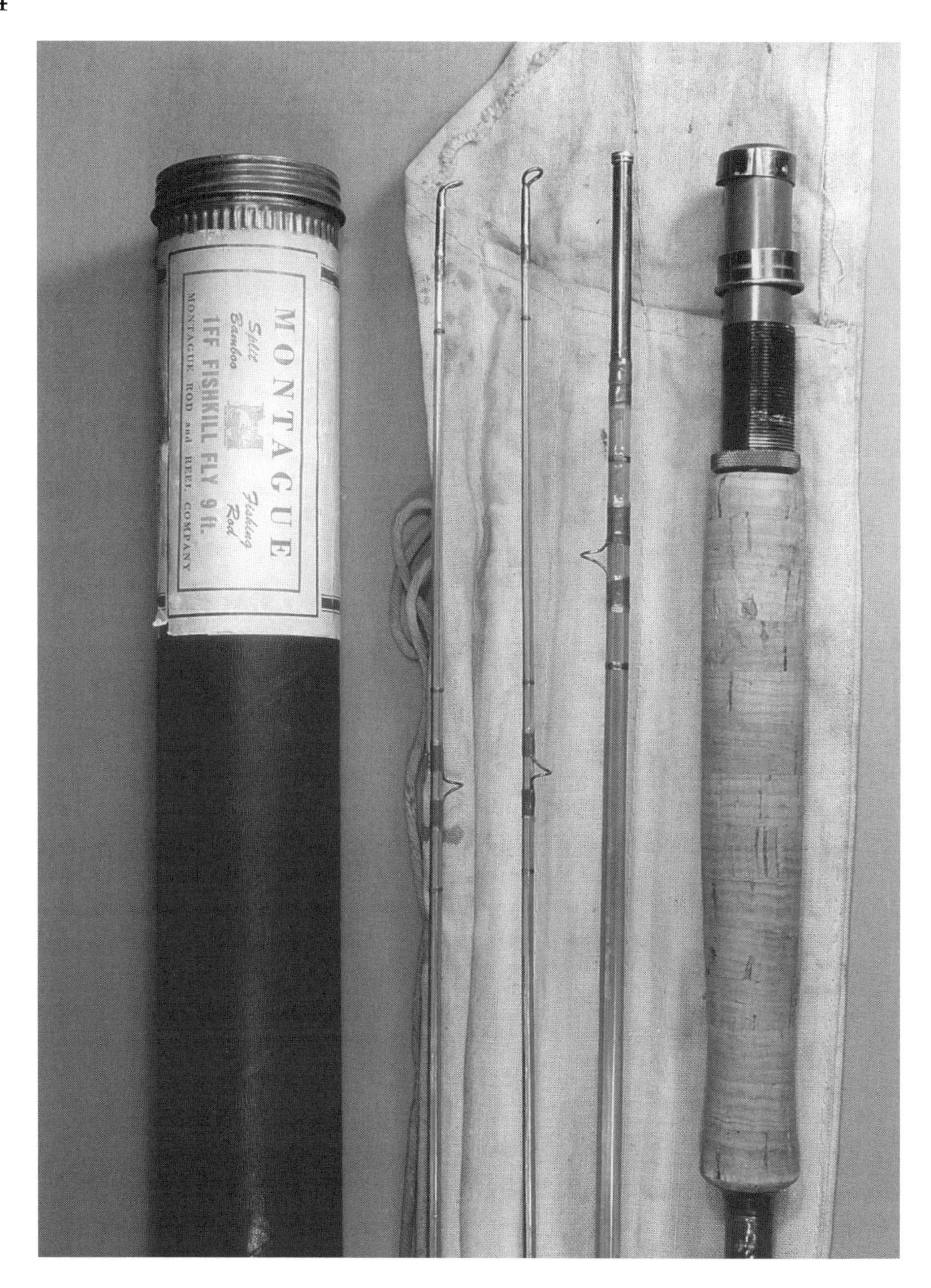

An admirable Montague *Fishkill* bamboo fly rod. The ferrules and reel seat hardware are blued nickel-silver, and the reel seat insert is a teal green plastic made to complement the green guide wraps. It is in very-good, close to excellent condition — in the original cloth bag and cardboard fiber tube. These better quality Montagues are quite alluring and very collectible (yet the value is relatively low due to the great numbers produced).

Compact *R. L. Winston* fiberglass fly rod is pictured here next to a brace of hatchery trout. This is an outstanding three-piece, 7 1/2 foot model made in Montana during the early 1980s.

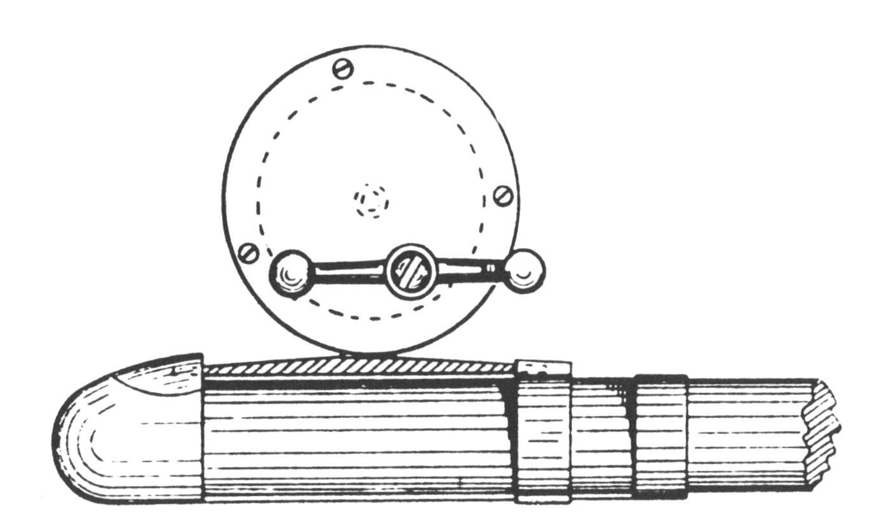

It is interesting to see the similarity between an original Fred Devine "slide-ring reel plate holder" patented in 1885 and the Winston reel seat above. One would merely have to recognize the longevity of Devine's invention to consider it a success — and the influence of his design is apparent in a rod constructed nearly 100 years later!

Shakespeare #1360 *Silver Creek* bamboo fly rod in very good condition. This 9 foot model is a better grade Shakespeare, fitted with nickel-silver ferrules, rather than the plated ferrules found on many later Shakespeare rods. Both tips are full length and the ferrules are tight and functional — attributes not always present on some mass-produced, so-called factory bamboo fly rods.

In our computerized, mechanized society it is nice to know that a few traditional art forms endure. Maine to Oregon, in Canada, Europe, in small shops around the globe — individual bamboo rod builders keep that craft alive and well. Rod maker Lyle Hand is pictured above splitting the cane. With his knife clamped in a vise, a partial culm is carefully pushed against the stationary blade (forming strips). Next, all nodes are sanded and the six numbered strips are set aside to be planed at a later time.

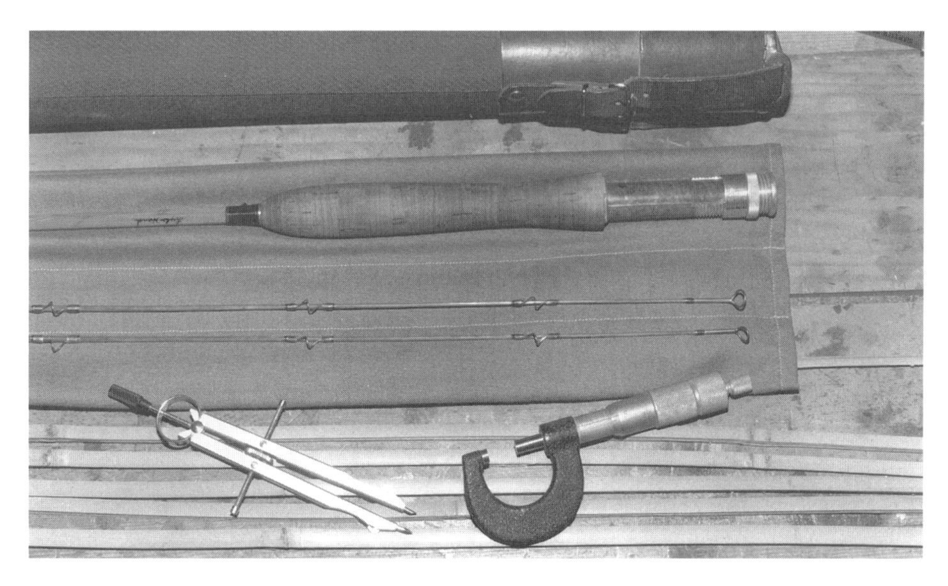

A fast, dry fly rod (7 1/2 feet) from the Bellingham, Washington shop of Lyle Hand. Lyle also produces fine, practical trout nets from a variety of woods.

Talented, contemporary bamboo rod craftsman Steve Gobin is pictured here working at the planing form. He apprenticed under Daryll Whitehead of Seattle, Washington. Steve is also considered to be one of the world's top makers of traditional Atlantic salmon flies. (Mike Malloy Photo)

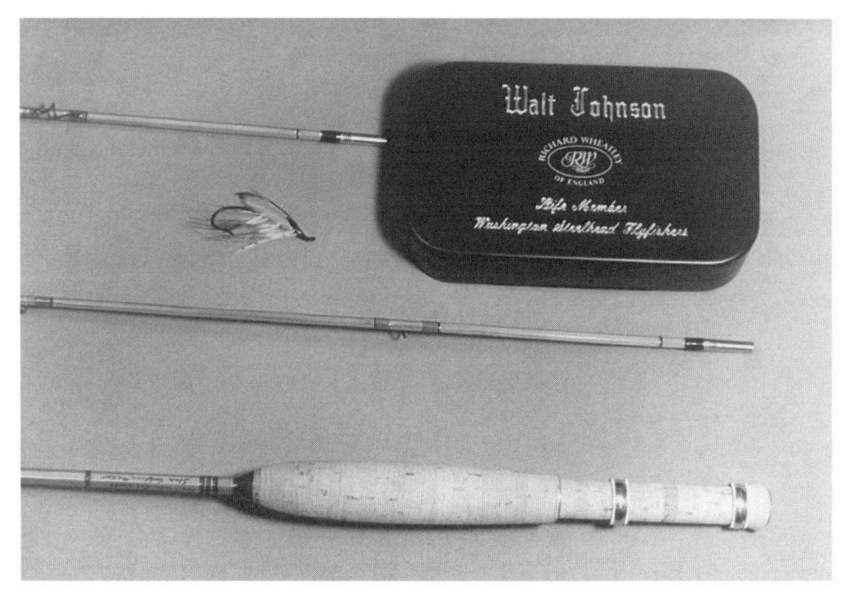

The midge rod pictured above was custom made by Steve Gobin (Quilceda Rod Works) and presented to veteran steelhead angler Walt Johnson.

Bait Casting Rods

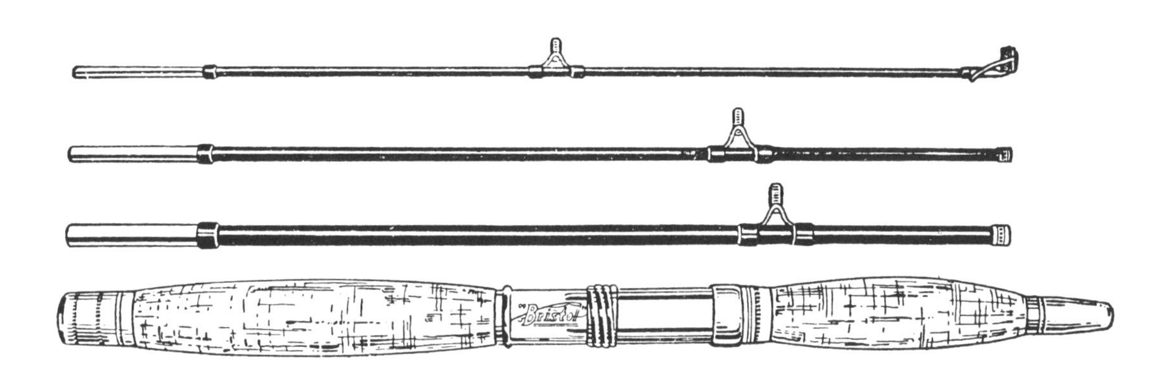

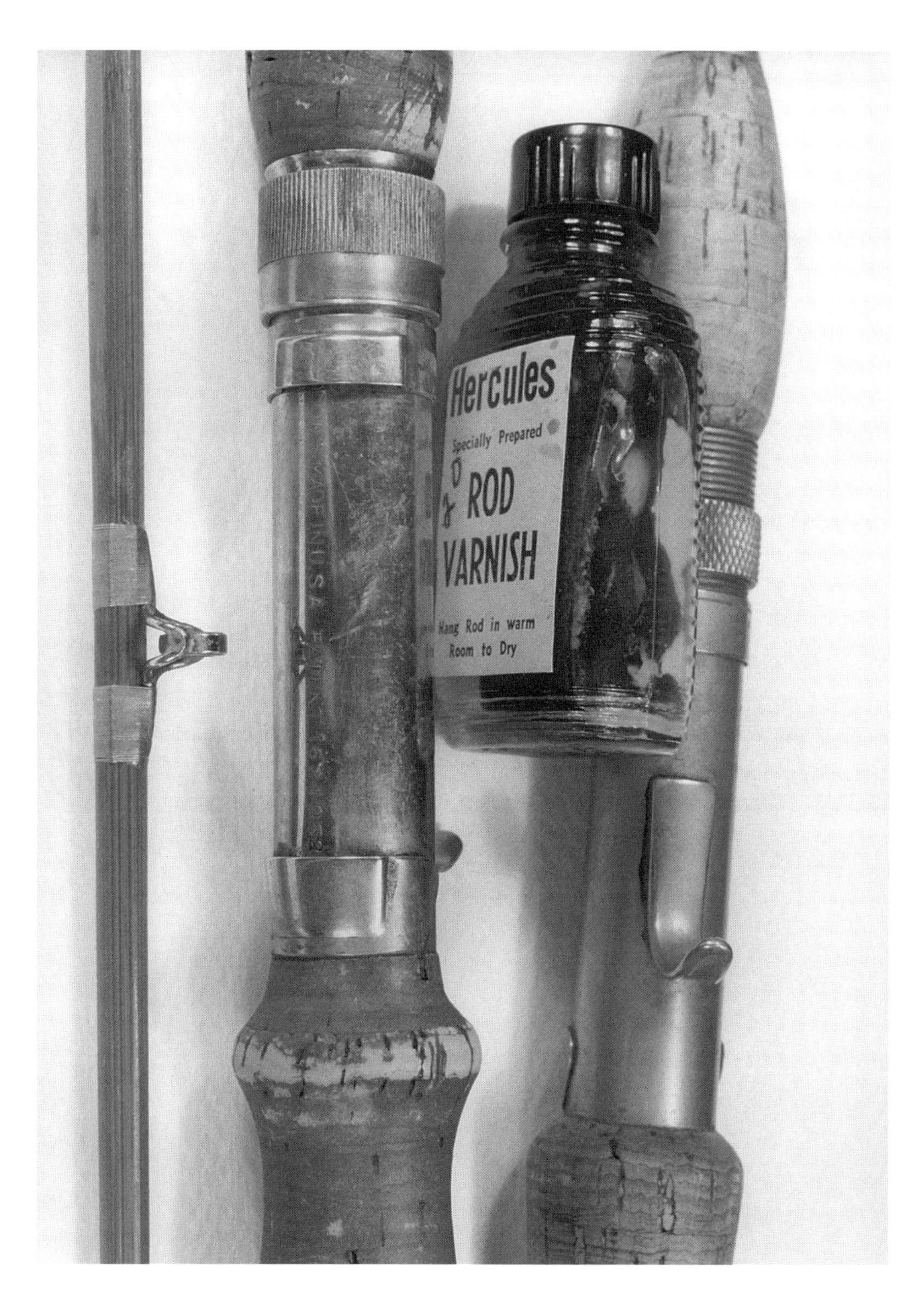

A close-up of Heddon's famous reel seat (patent #1,624,052) an exquisite nickel-silver screw-lock style found on the Michigan maker's bait casting rods during the 1930 to 1940 era.

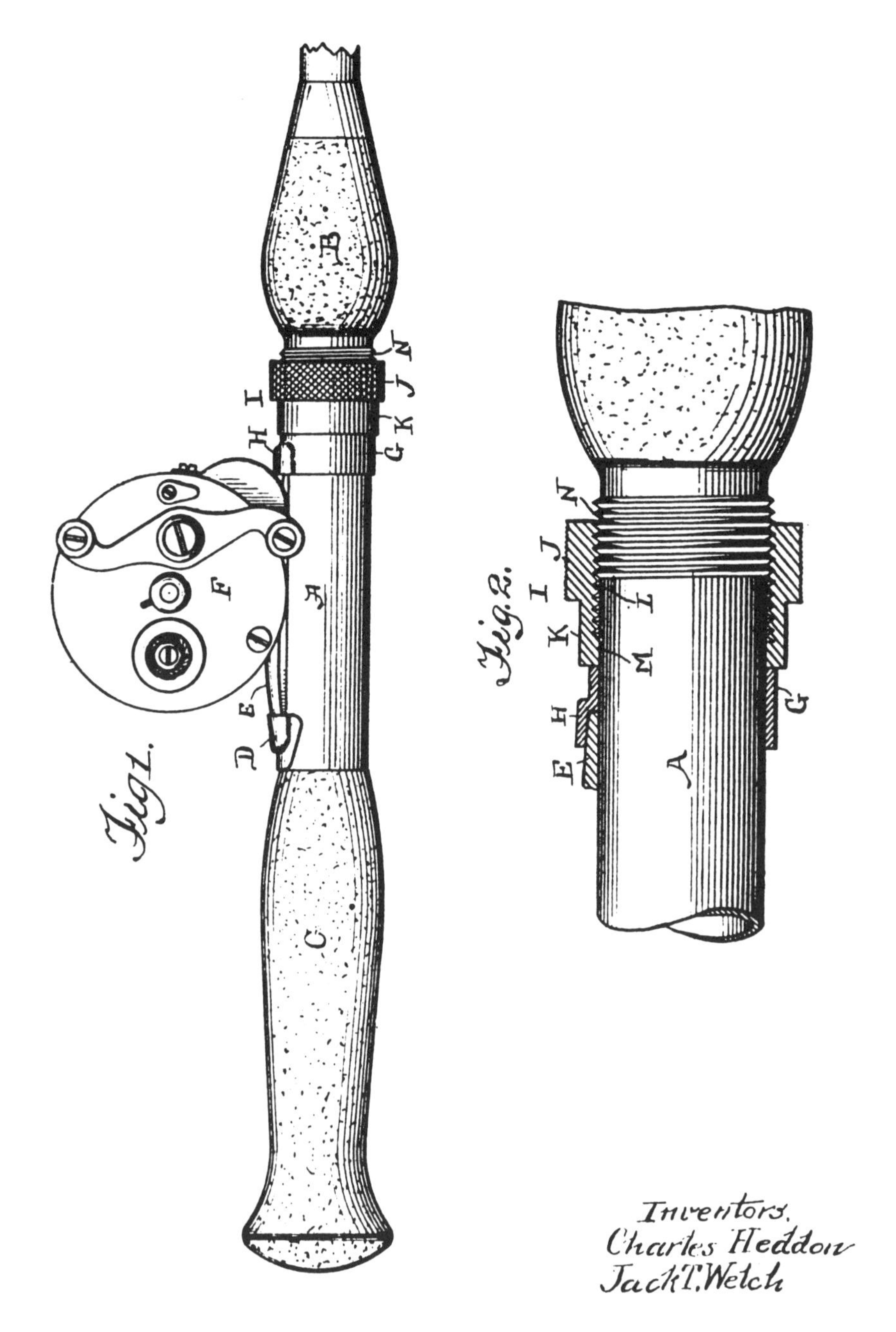

Charles Heddon and Jack Welch were the inventors of patent #1,624,052 which was assigned to the James Heddon Corporation in 1927. The primary feature of this reel seat mechanism is the function of a hooded sliding clamping ring (**G**) which is adapted to be moved into position to secure the reel base plate (foot) by means of an adjustable, threaded follower ring consisting of an outwardly enlarged knurled portion (**J**) and a reduced portion (**K**). As stated in the patent application . . . *a turning of the adjustable follower ring will cause the same to move rearwardly carrying with it the clamping ring which will slide smoothly and closely upon the barrel until moved to a position to engage and hold the reel in place.*

A very early Heddon bait casting reel seat — a design almost identical to the 1890 "reel fastener" invented by John Landman of Brooklyn, New York.

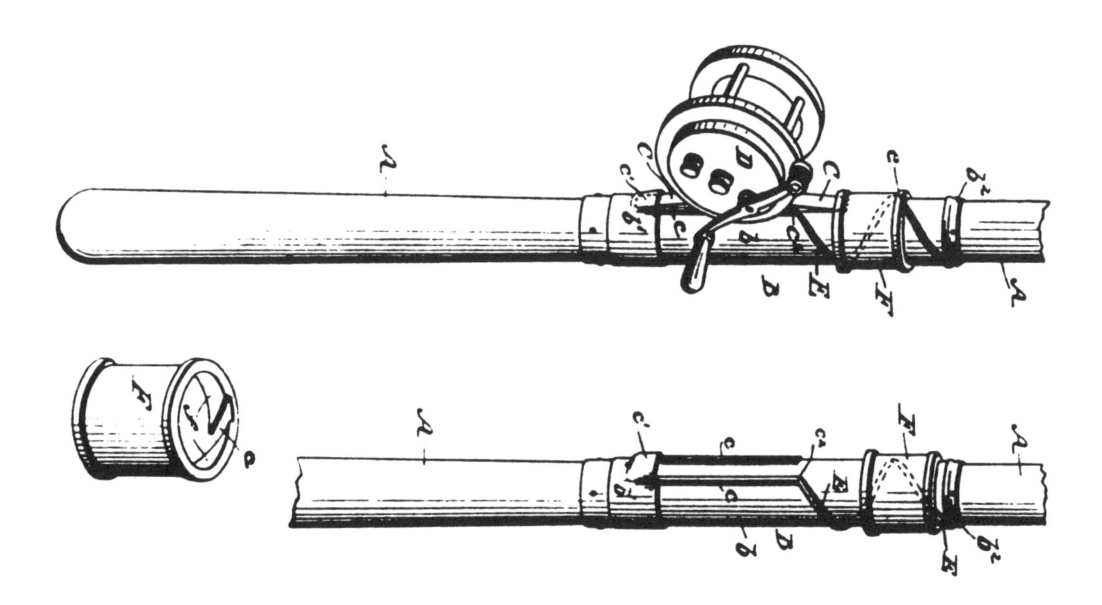

A portion of the Landman "reel fastener" patent. A spiral-flange (**E**) forms a screw-thread to which is fitted a fastening-nut (**F**). The fastening nut has an interior rib portion so as to fit the spiral-flange and cause the nut, when turned, to traverse the reel seat longitudinally — thus locking the reel in place.

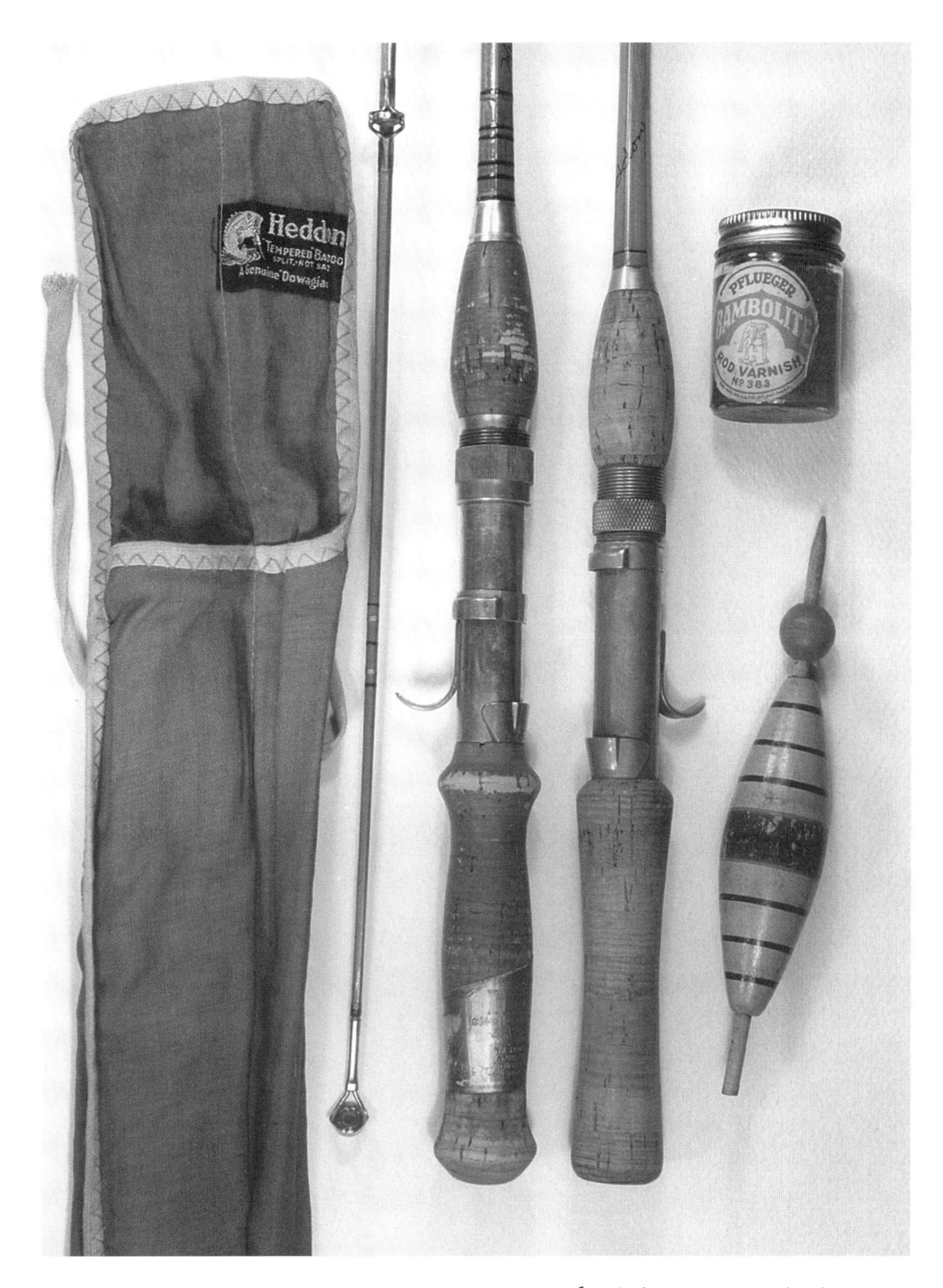

Two nice Heddon cane bait casting rods — on the left, an unmarked two-piece model with its original cloth bag. The other, a one-piece model #2A-5-M (medium action). Both rods are five feet long and are equipped with what Heddon called "crystal agate" guides and top.

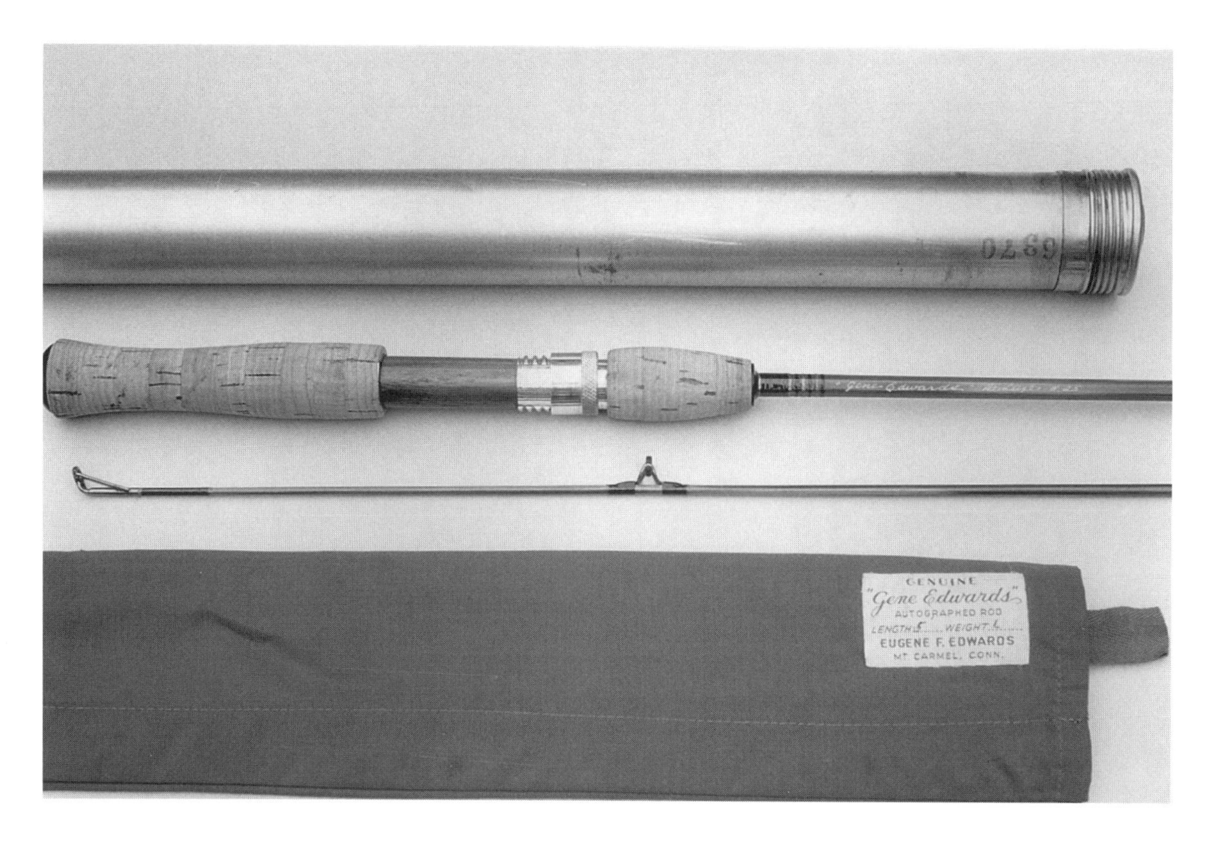

Gene Edwards *Deluxe* #25 two-piece bamboo bait casting rod built in Mt. Carmel, Connecticut. This light, 5 foot rod was found in its original bag and case.

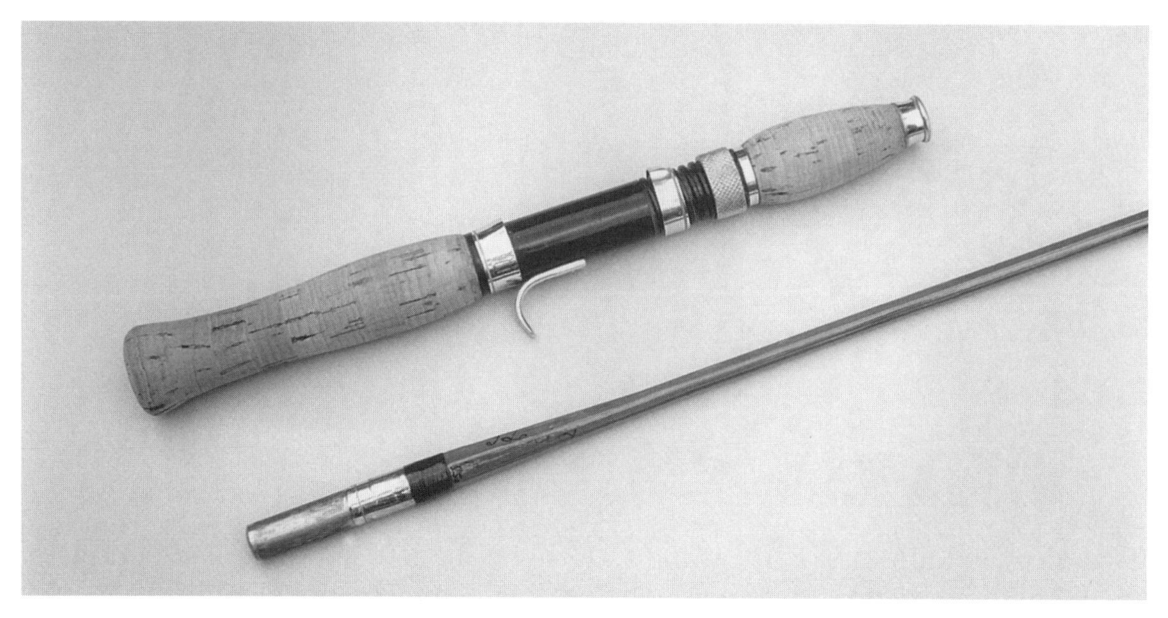

The Heddon #850-R one-piece, 6 foot bamboo casting rod with a detachable handle — an extra-light action model designed for 1/4 to 3/8 oz. lures.

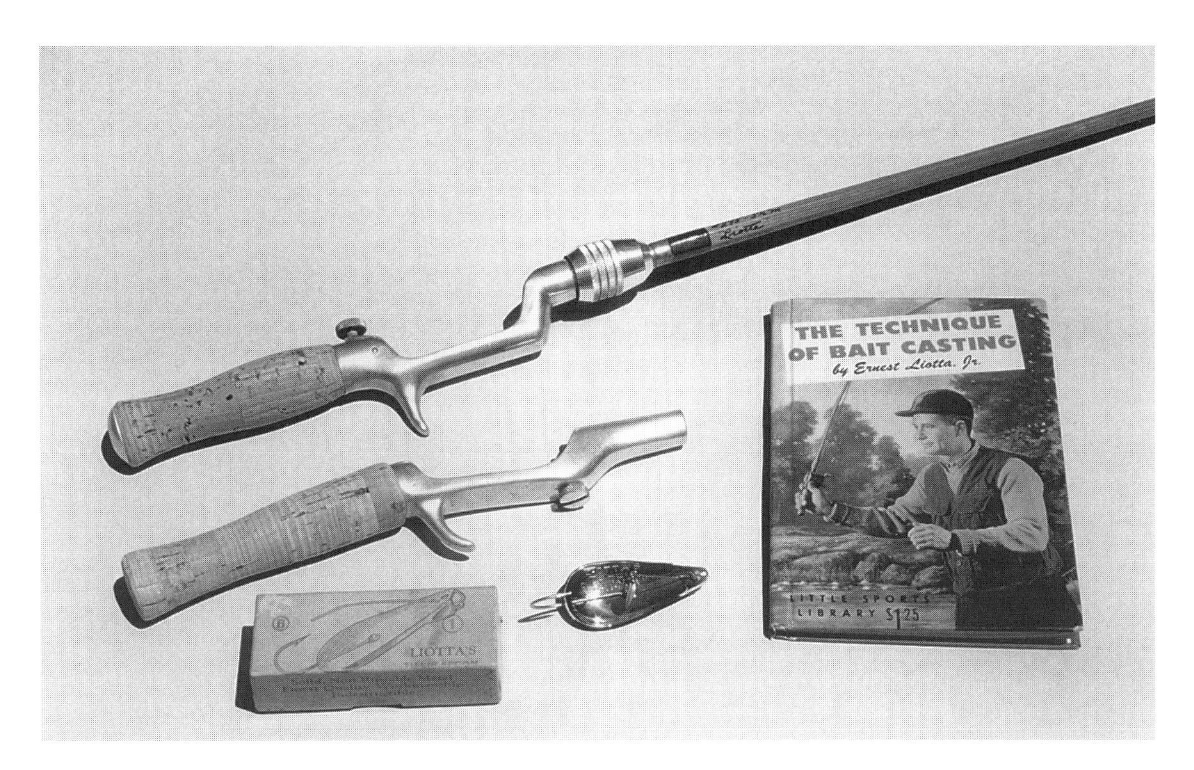

A *Liotta Model* #275 bamboo bait casting rod marketed by NARMCO, later known as Conolon (National Rod Manufacturing Co.). This is a curious 5 1/2 foot, one-piece rod. The handle is similar to those produced by True Temper of Cleveland, Ohio. The bamboo section of the rod may have been crafted by a local Cleveland rod maker. Ernest Liotta Jr. was a famous tournament caster from Ohio.

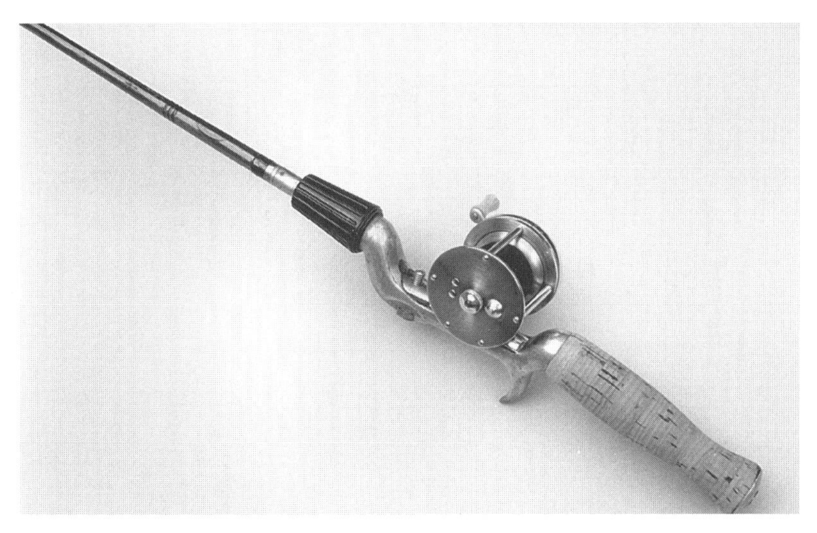

Shakespeare *Tony Accetta Model* bamboo bait casting rod circa 1940. A better quality Shakespeare equipped with agate guides and a detachable handle. Shakespeare offered a series of rods named after this well-known tournament caster.

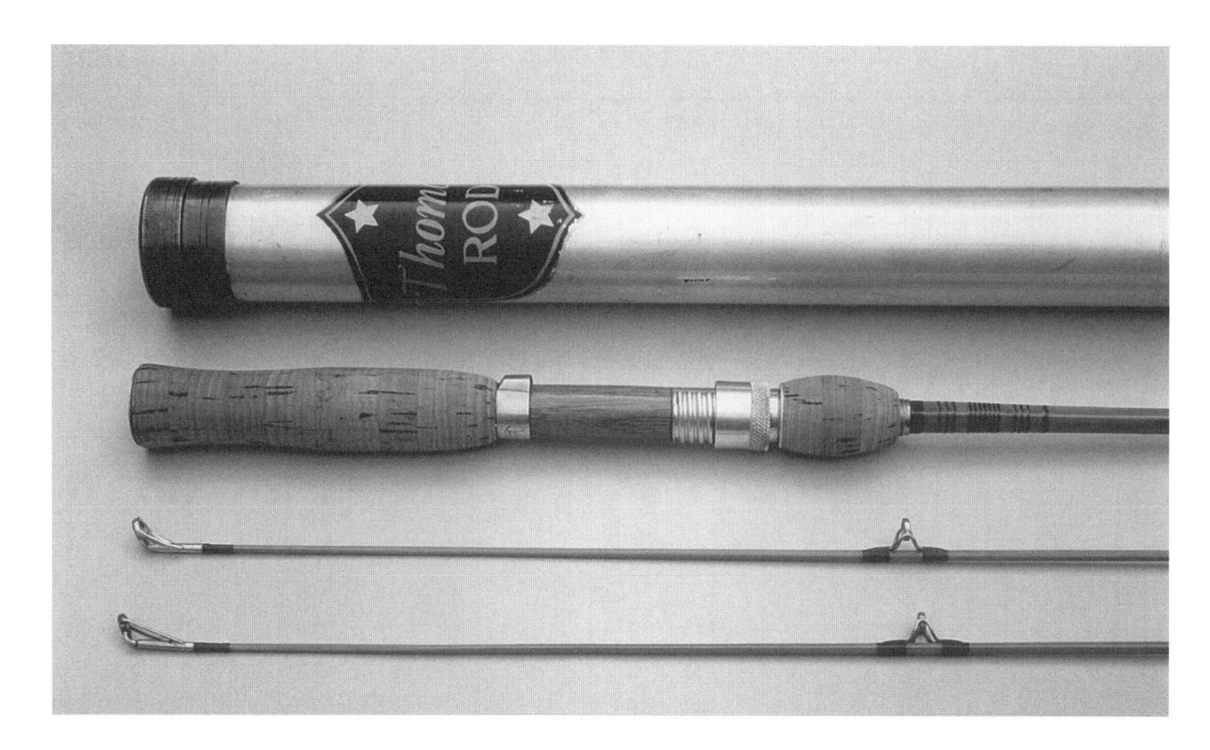

F.E. Thomas *Special* — a scarce 6 foot, two-piece bamboo bait caster complete with two tips. This deluxe rod has a screw-lock reel seat with wood insert, and is a staggered-ferrule design. It was discovered in excellent condition, accompanied by the original bag and case. Made in Bangor, Maine circa 1930.

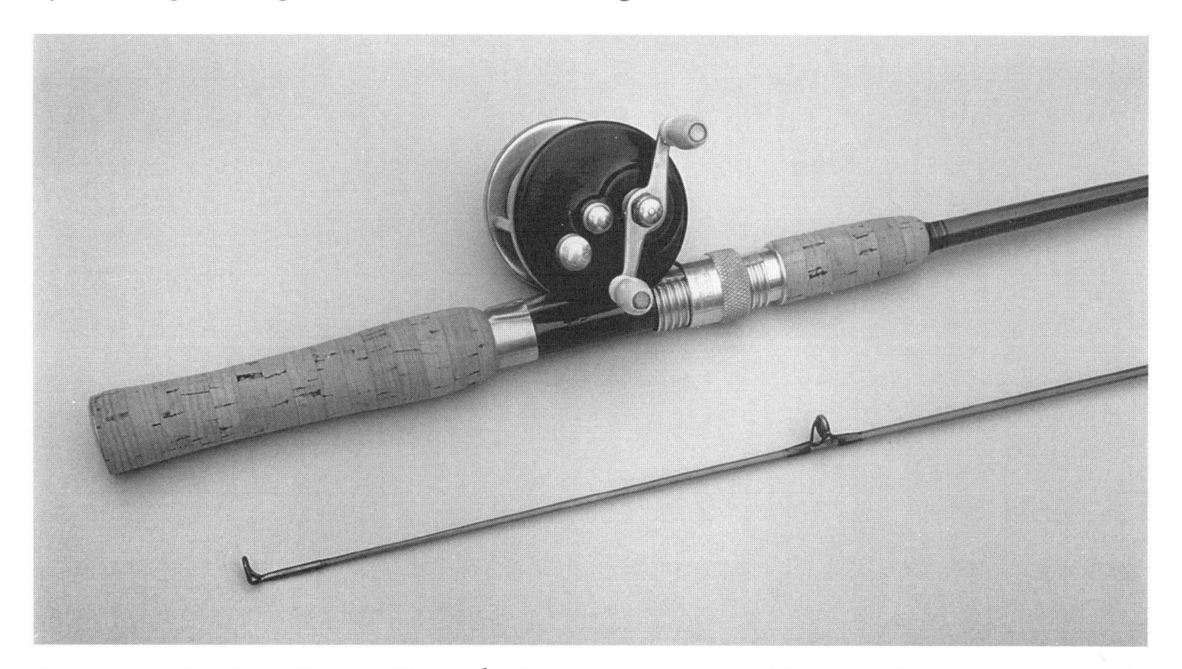

A spectacular E. F. Payne Co. light bait casting rod of 5 feet. Payne casting rods are highly collectible. This is a two-piece model with agate guides.

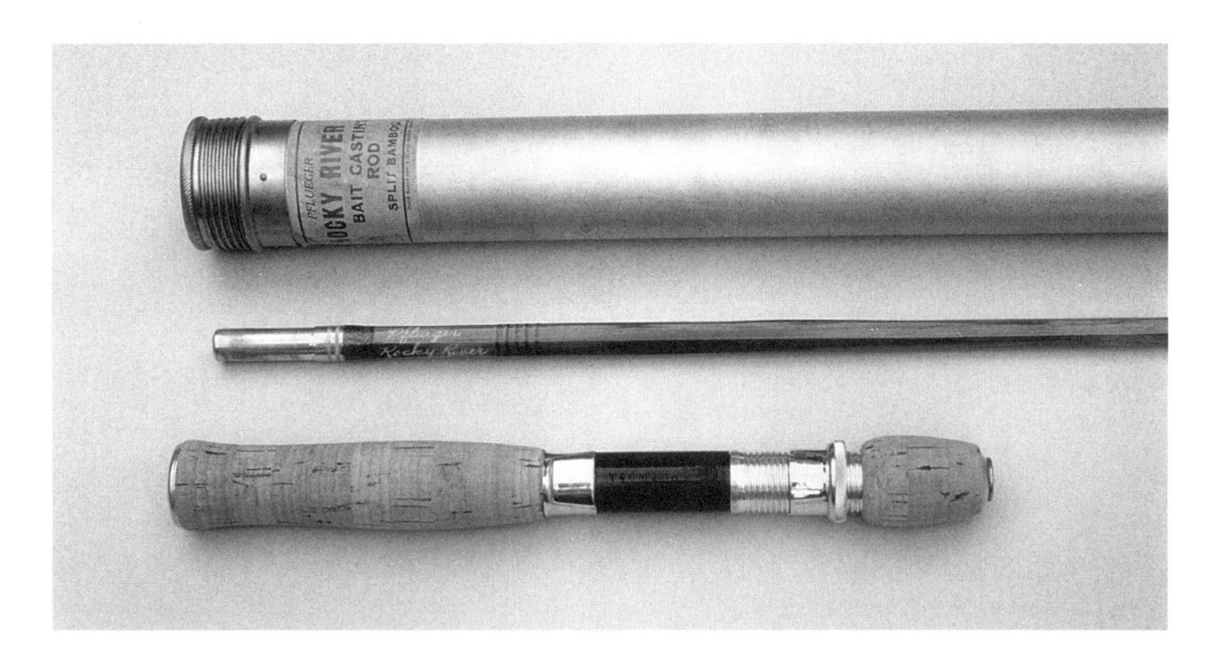

Pflueger *Rocky River* bamboo bait casting rod — 5 feet, one-piece with a detachable handle. Pflueger split-bamboo rods are an unusual find. Pflueger named their rods and reels after Ohio locales, i.e. Akron reel, Norka reel (Akron spelled backward!). Rocky River is a small stream west of Cleveland.

Early San Francisco Winston 7 foot, two-piece bait caster — followed by a rare E.C. Powell 6 foot, two-piece model made in Marysville, California. Both rods are combined with Meek casting reels. The Lew Stoner built Winston (serial #3536) is equipped with a reel seat locking band and threaded jam nut bearing the Feb. 15, 1927 patent attributable to Wes Jordan.

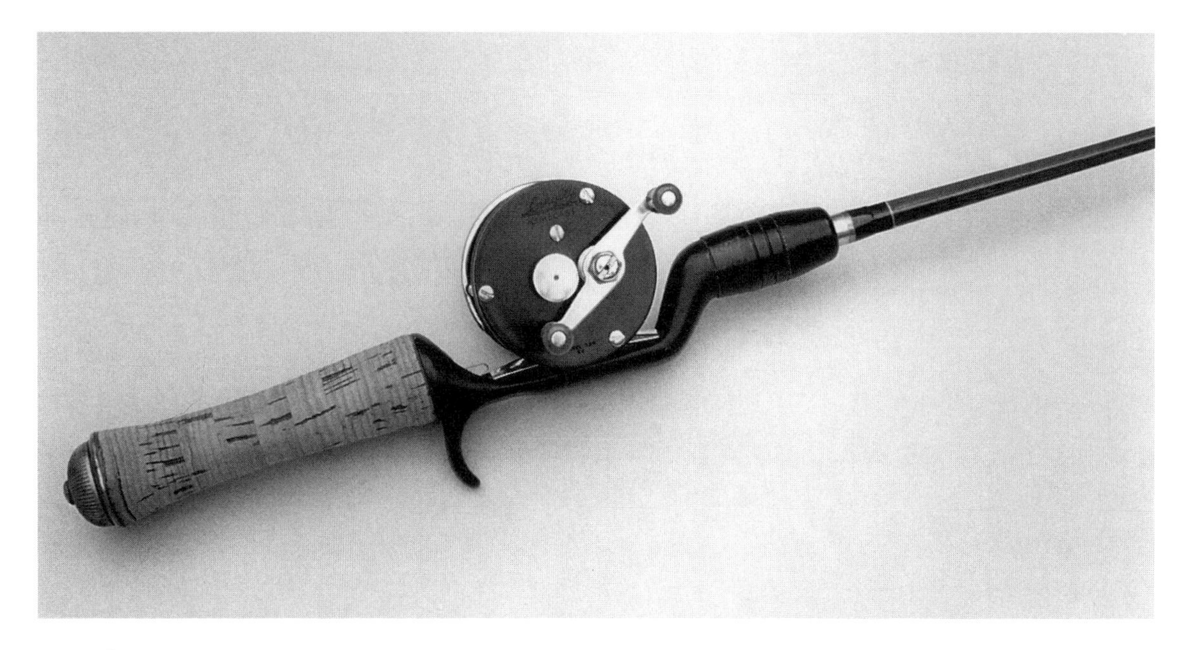

Wright & McGill *Paramount* 6 foot. two-piece bamboo bait casting rod with detachable handle. The reel seat locking mechanism is engaged by means of a screw-design butt cap — based loosely on the same principle as the Wright & McGill *Granger* fly rod reel seat.

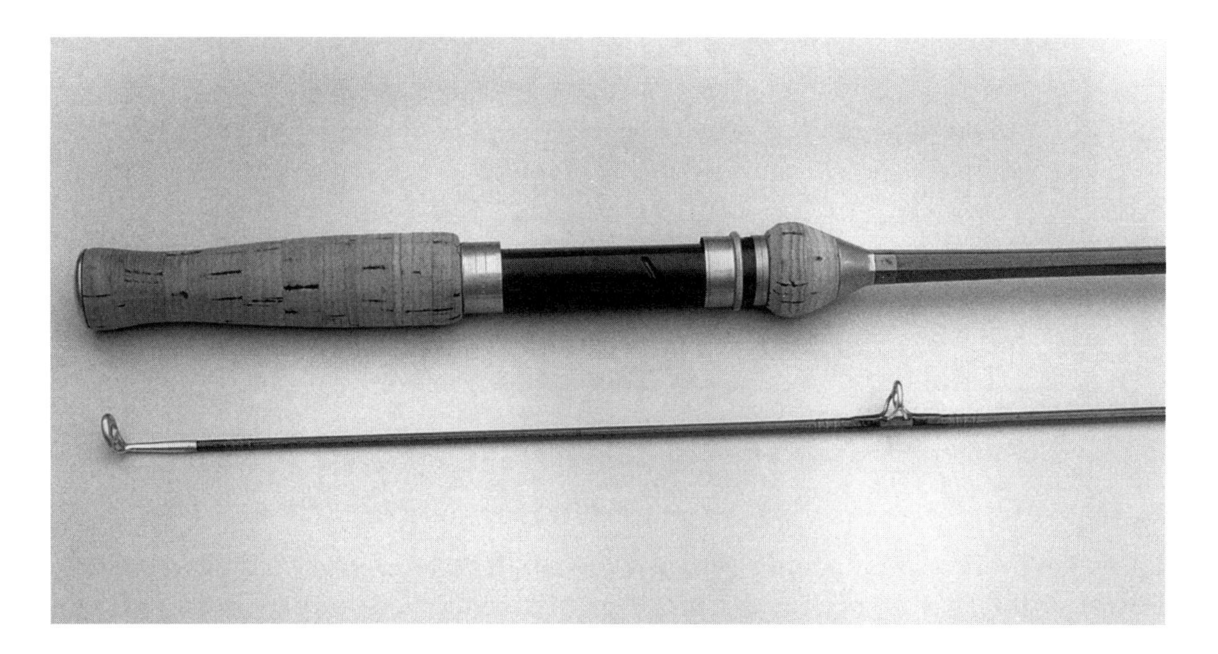

The distinctive Goodwin Granger 6 foot *Granger Deluxe* bait casting rod made in Colorado — a classic two-piece rod designed to cast 3/8 to 5/8 oz. lures.

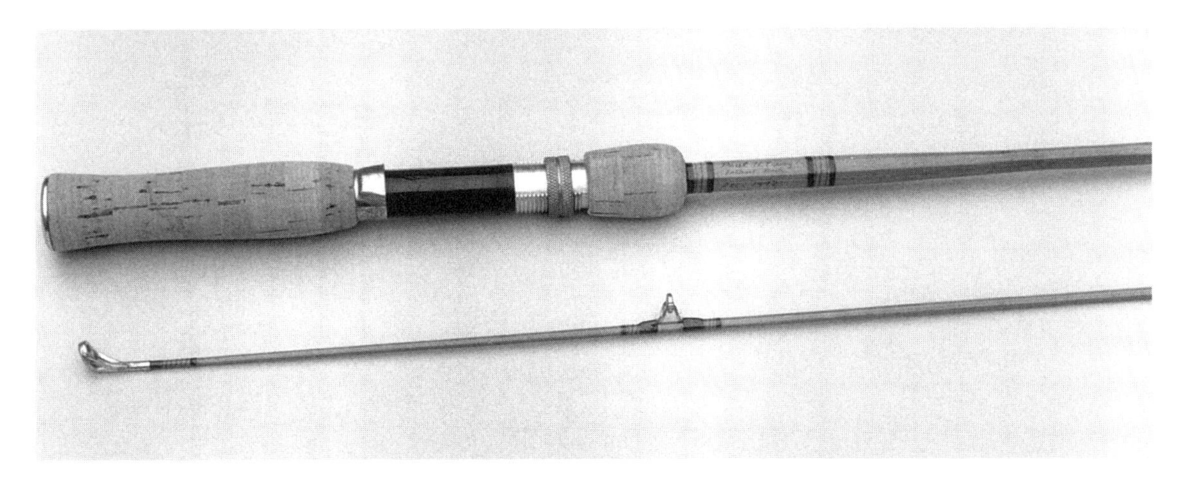

Paul Young 6 1/2′ bamboo bait caster expertly refinished by Bob Summers. This two-piece rod was made in 1942 and features staggered ferrules.

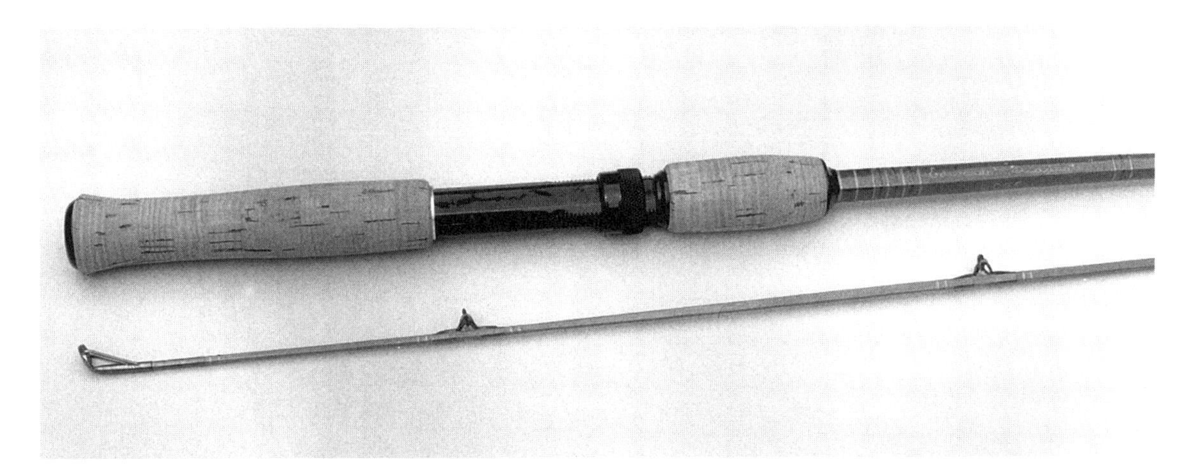

Edwards *Quadrate* #6525 two-piece bait caster. This four-strip, 5 1/2 foot rod is extremely light and quite attractive — it is in excellent original condition.

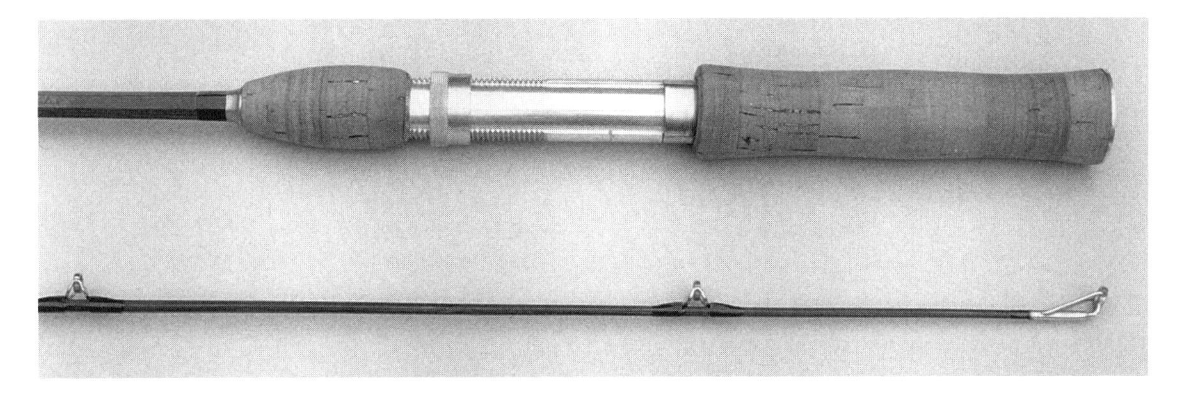

Orvis impregnated bamboo casting rod from the 1950s. It is a 6 foot model of the staggered ferrule design (two-piece with one tip). For 3/8 oz. lures.

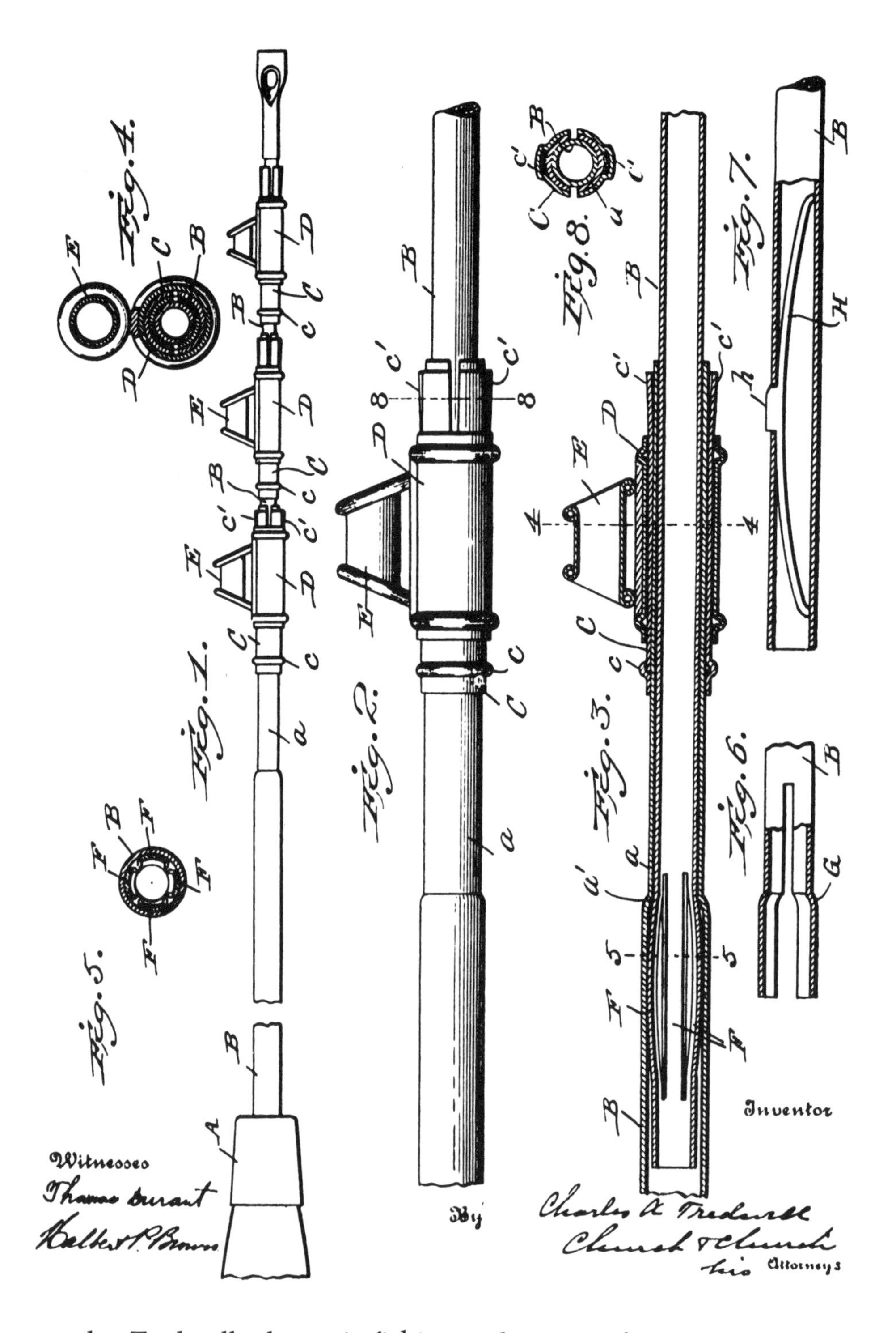

The complex Tredwell telescopic fishing rod patent of June 10, 1913 (assigned to the Horton Manufacturing Company of Bristol, Conn.). Tredwell suggested that the sliding sleeve (**D**) with guide (**E**) attached, could be forcibly withdrawn from the ferrule to permit substitution of a new or different sleeve/guide as desired by the angler.

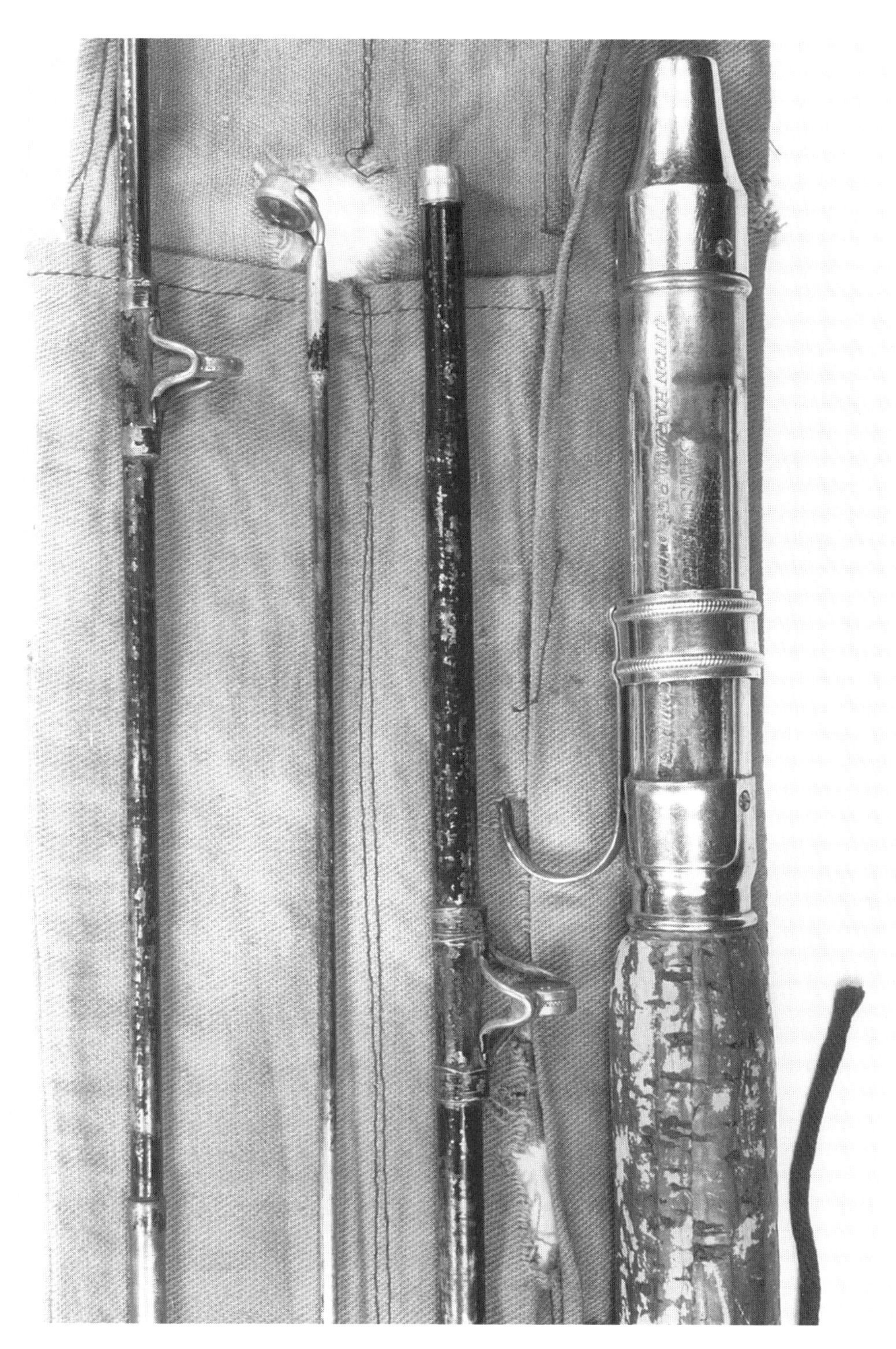

Union Hardware Co. of Torrington, Connecticut was the manufacturer of this *Samson* tubular steel bait casting rod. It is a four-piece model finished black, with agate guides and brass ferrules. The handle detaches as a result of a joint at the top of the reel seat — similar to the Tredwell patent of 1905.

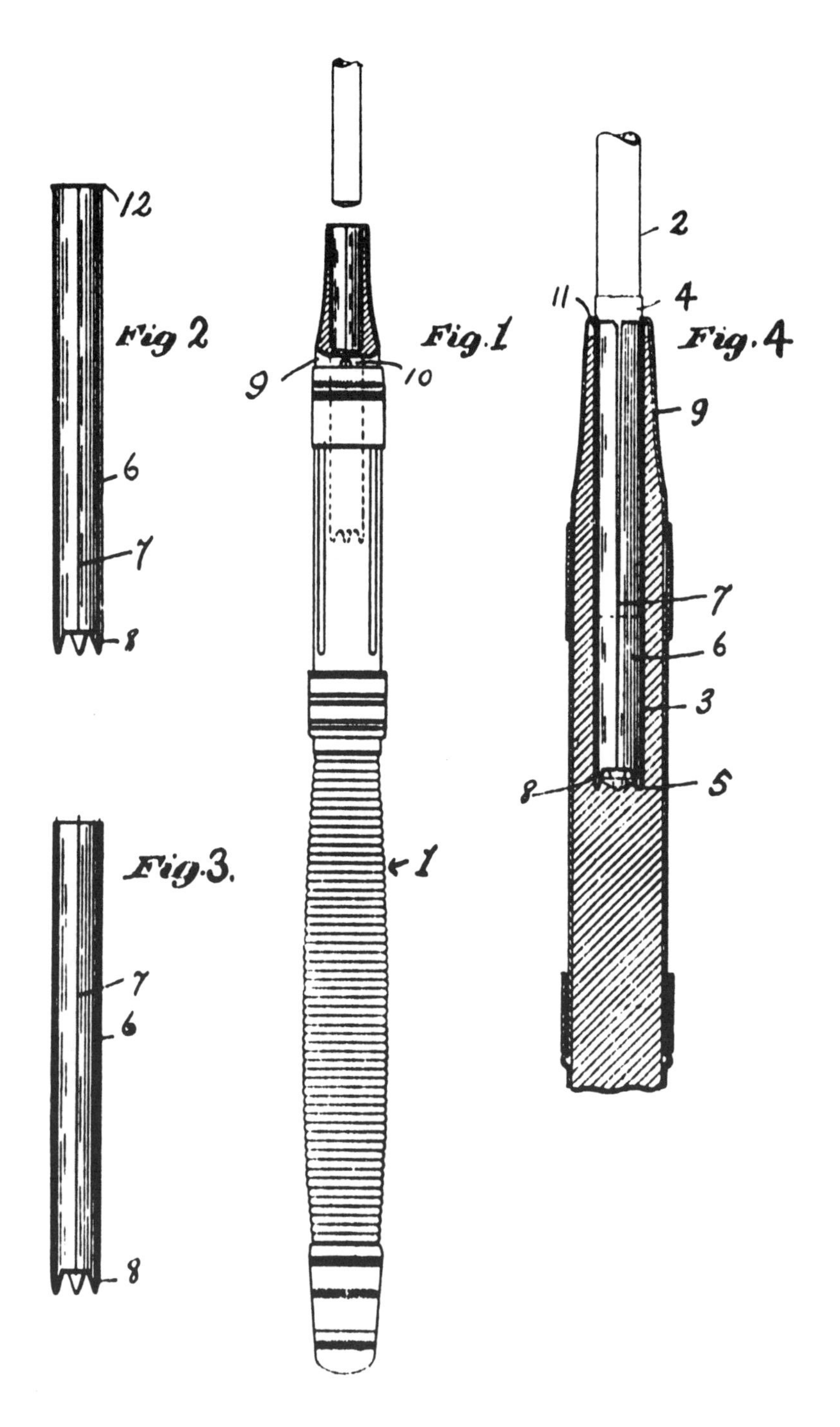

The Charles Tredwell patent drawing depicting an improved joint socket (Sept. 19, 1905). In Tredwell's own words . . . *The object of the present invention is to provide an improved socket for the handle or grip of such a construction that it will receive and hold, with the desired frictional contact, the ends of sections which may vary slightly in diameter* . . . This is accomplished by means of an expanding thimble (**part 6**) formed from rolled sheet steel but not united (**seam 7**), whereby the thimble may be free to expand. Thus the socket can accept ferrules of varying diameter.

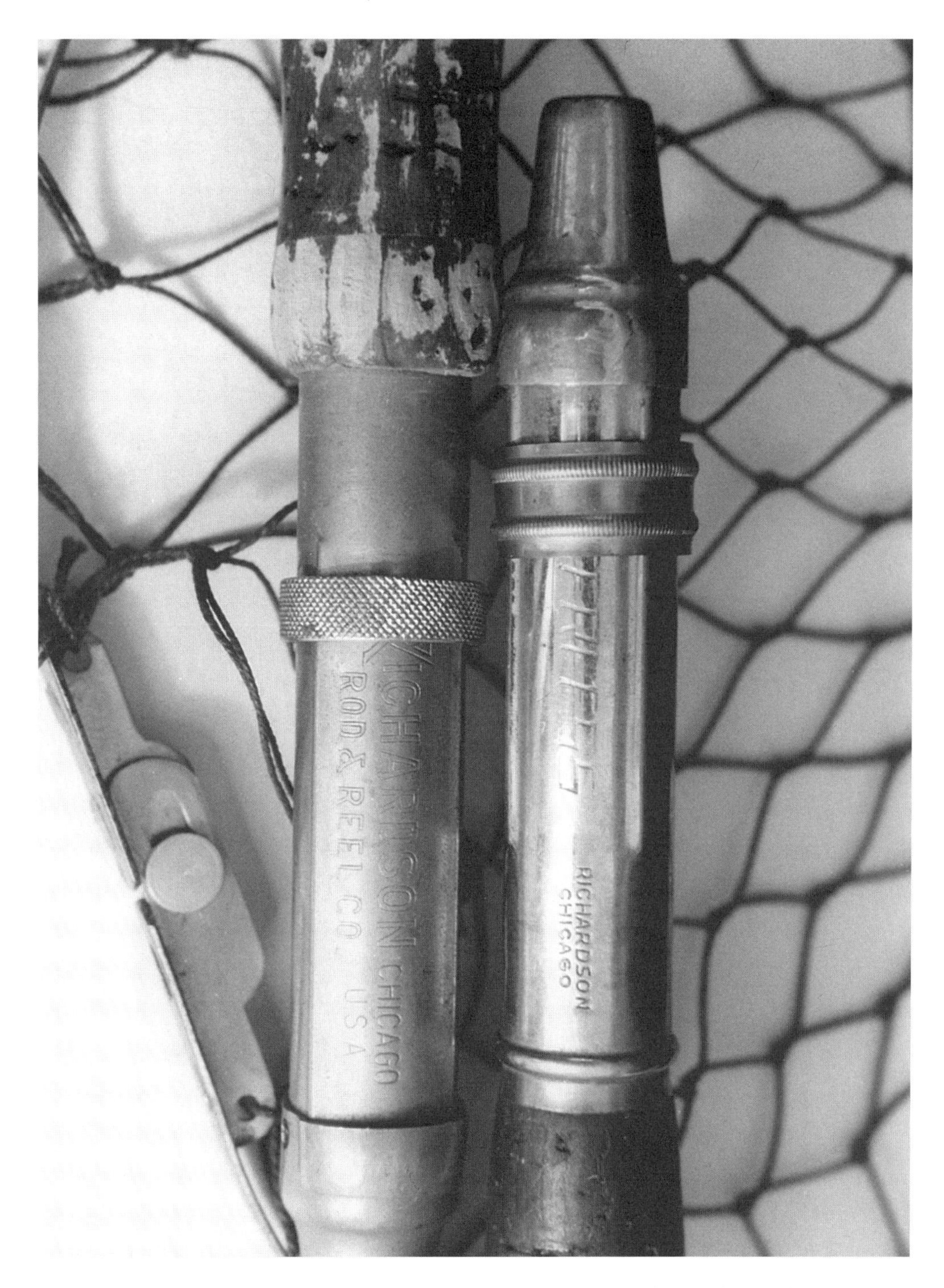

The Richardson Rod & Reel Co. of Chicago was an early maker of steel products including durable fishing rods, fishing nets, and roller skates. Two examples of Richardson reel seats are pictured here. The popular *Peerless* model combination rod is shown along with a Richardson *Harrimac* design collapsible steel trout net — all circa 1925.

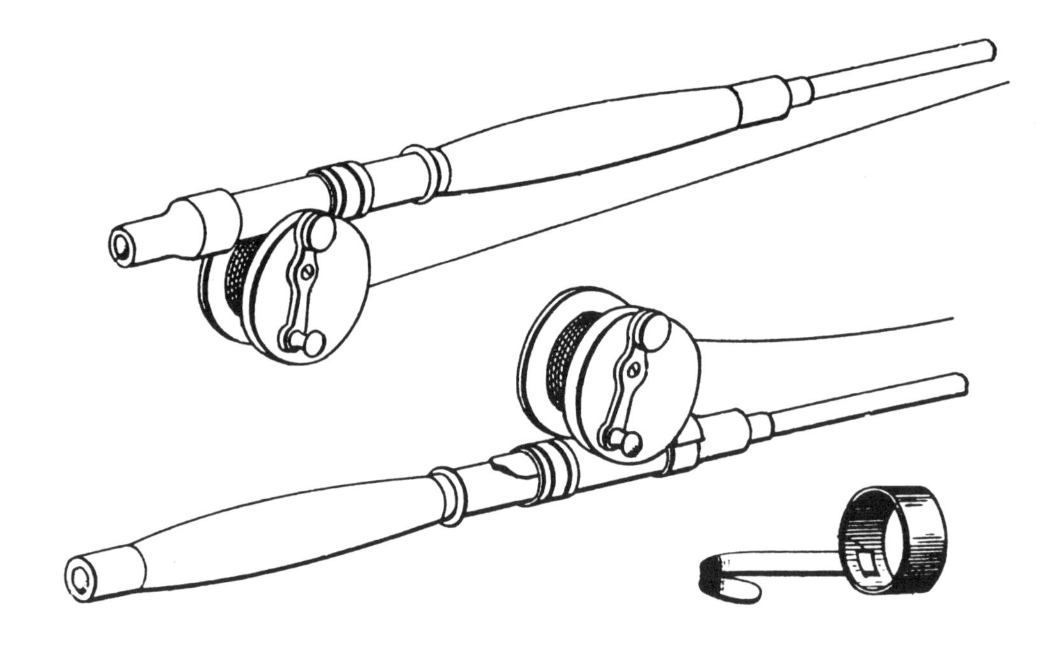

Two other innovations created by Charles Tredwell for tubular steel rods. **(Top)** The reversible handle utilized in converting a fly rod to a bait casting rod was patented in 1912. **(Bottom)** The early trigger or pistol-finger grip was patented in 1903. This device incorporated a sliding ring for retaining the fishing reel. Both patents were assigned to The Horton Manufacturing Co.

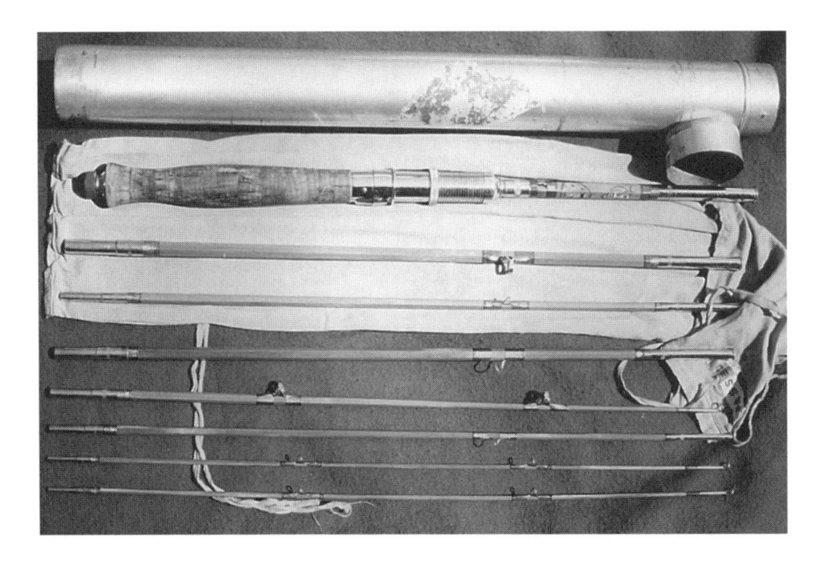

A good example of how the reversible handle design endured for many years. This eight-piece bamboo combination rod (separate fly and bait casting sections with the same handle) was made in Japan circa 1955. It is collectible, but worth quite a bit less than most mass-produced American bamboo rods.

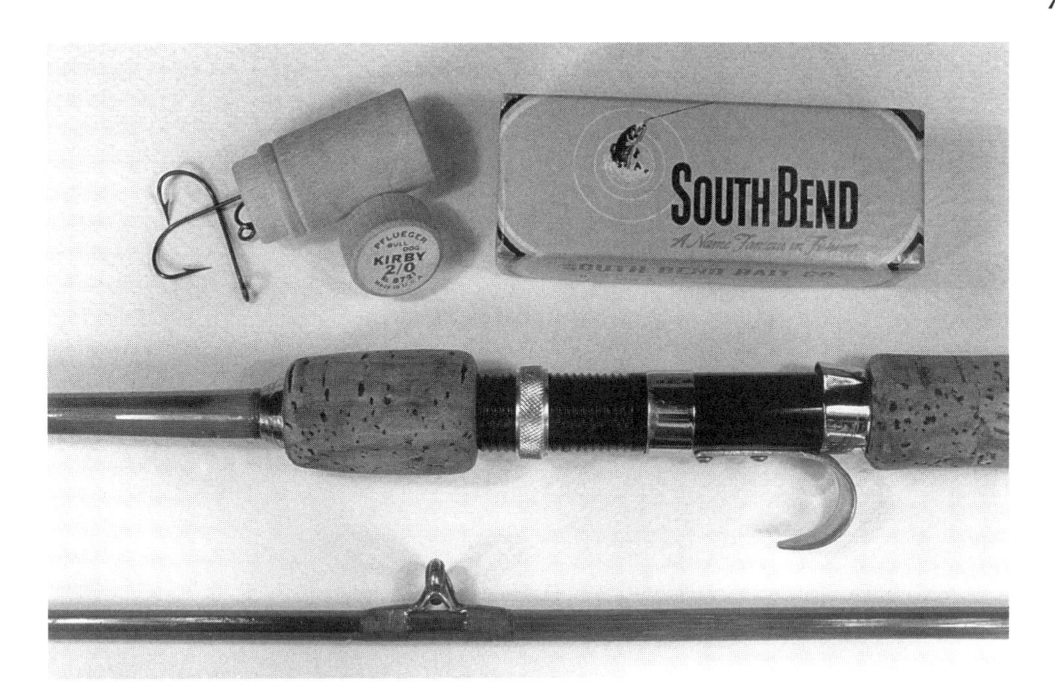

Horrocks-Ibbotson *Ontario* two-piece bait casting rod complete with agatine guides and black plastic reel seat circa 1950. An inexpensive rod, yet quite charming. This little 4 1/2 footer is a staggered ferrule design common on bait casting rods of this age (butt section shorter than tip section — a concept put forth to eliminate dampening of the action at the ferrule). Pictured with *South Bend* plug box and *Pflueger* wooden hook cylinder from the same era.

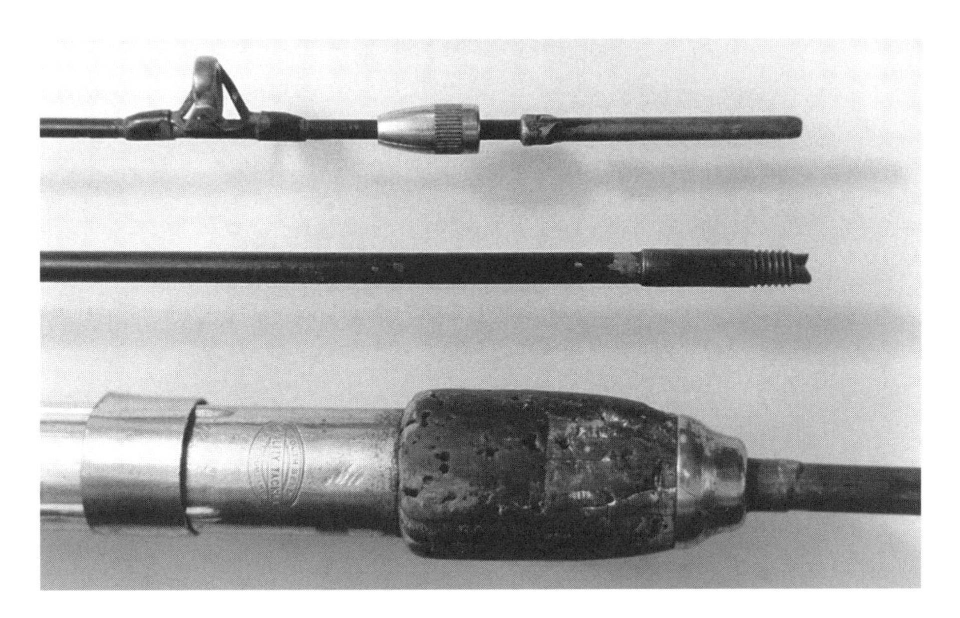

A unique steel bait casting rod made by *South Bend Bait Company* of Indiana. The brass male ferrule seats into the corresponding section and is secured by a locking threaded collar.

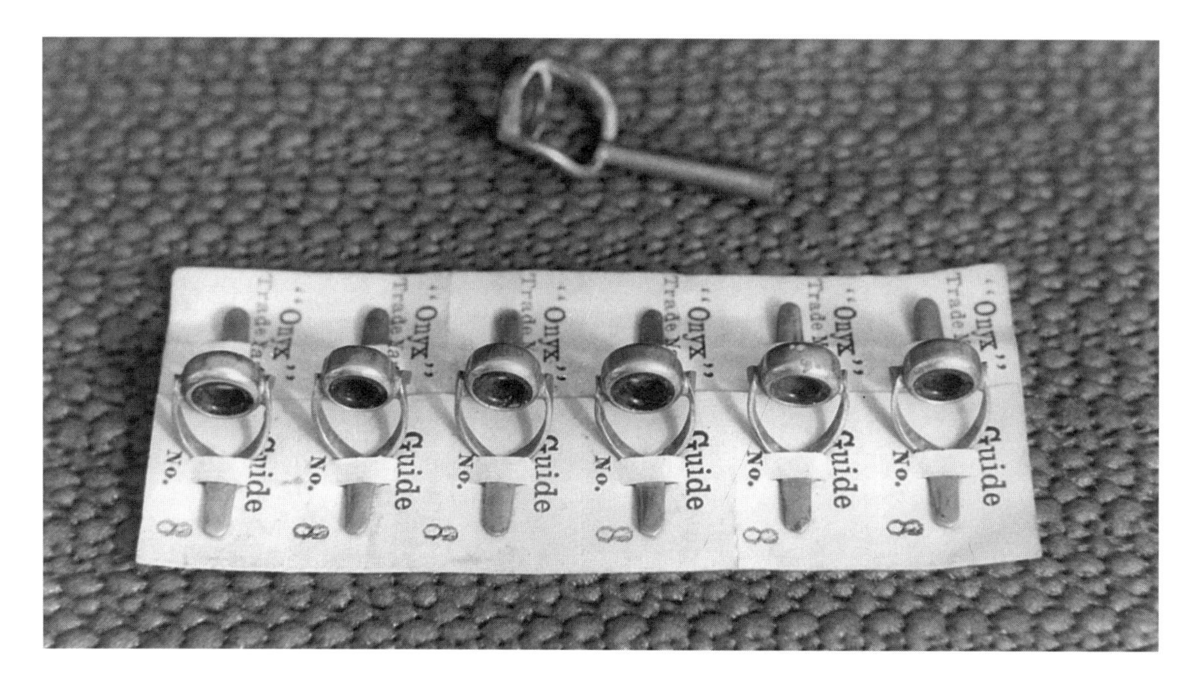

Genuine agate guides were typically reserved for a makers best bait casting rods. The *Onyx* guides pictured above are of similar quality and encircled by a nickel-silver frame. "Agateen" or "Agatine" was a term generally applied to other less expensive materials, including some ceramics. Agatine material was routinely inserted into chrome plated, rather than nickel-silver guides. This set of fine guides in the size 8 configuration would be a prize to the bamboo fly rod builder (for use as stripper guides).

A Horrocks-Ibbotson Co. reel seat utilized on both bait casting and light ocean rods. The knurled ring and sleeve can be moved along a track which accommodates the reel foot. Once the sleeve is adjusted to the correct position for a particular reel, the ring is turned to lock the sleeve against the track.

Ocean
&
Spinning Rods

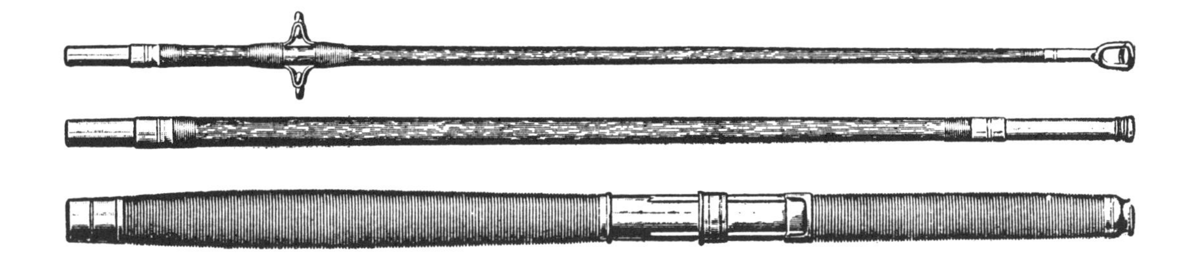

Close-up view of a high quality Edward Vom Hofe bamboo, big game trolling rod circa 1925 from New York. The rod was made to function well with a Vom Hofe reel such as the famous model 621. The reel seat is nickel-silver which is accompanied by a classic rattan wrapped grip and handle.

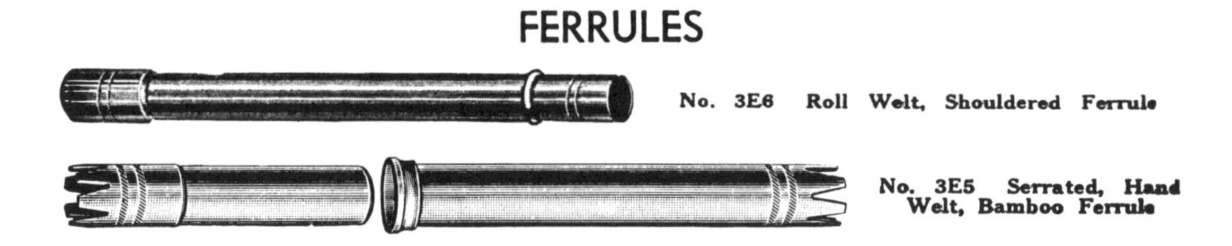

Old drawing illustrates ferrules of the type found on bamboo rods circa 1930.

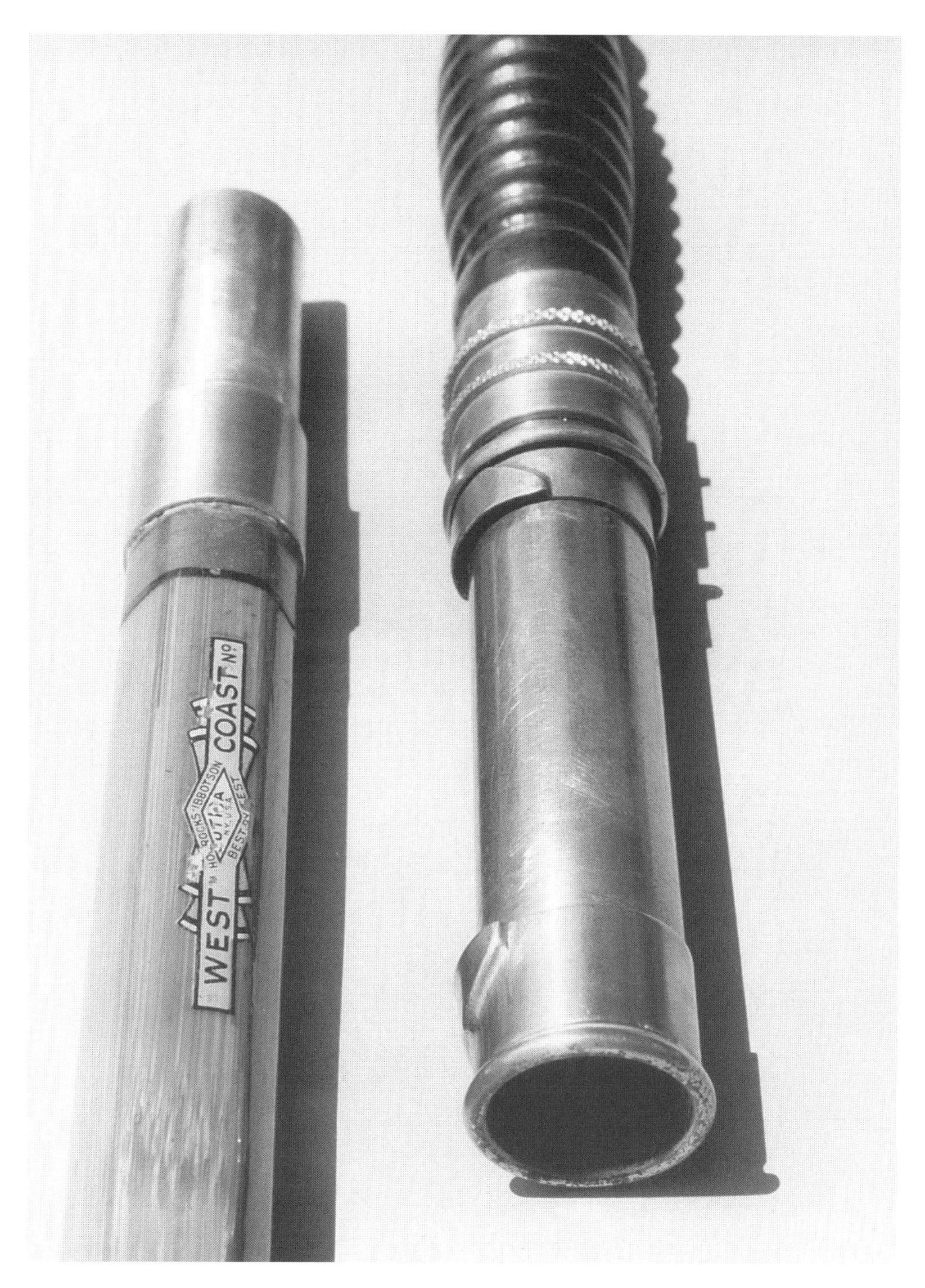

Horrocks-Ibbotson of Utica, New York sold this *West Coast* bamboo deep sea rod in the 1940 - 1950 era. The West Coast is one heavy duty piece of equipment with a stout tip section of 6 feet 8 inches long and a ferruled handle of 28 inches. This attractive collectible features a turned hardwood handle and double-sided agate guides.

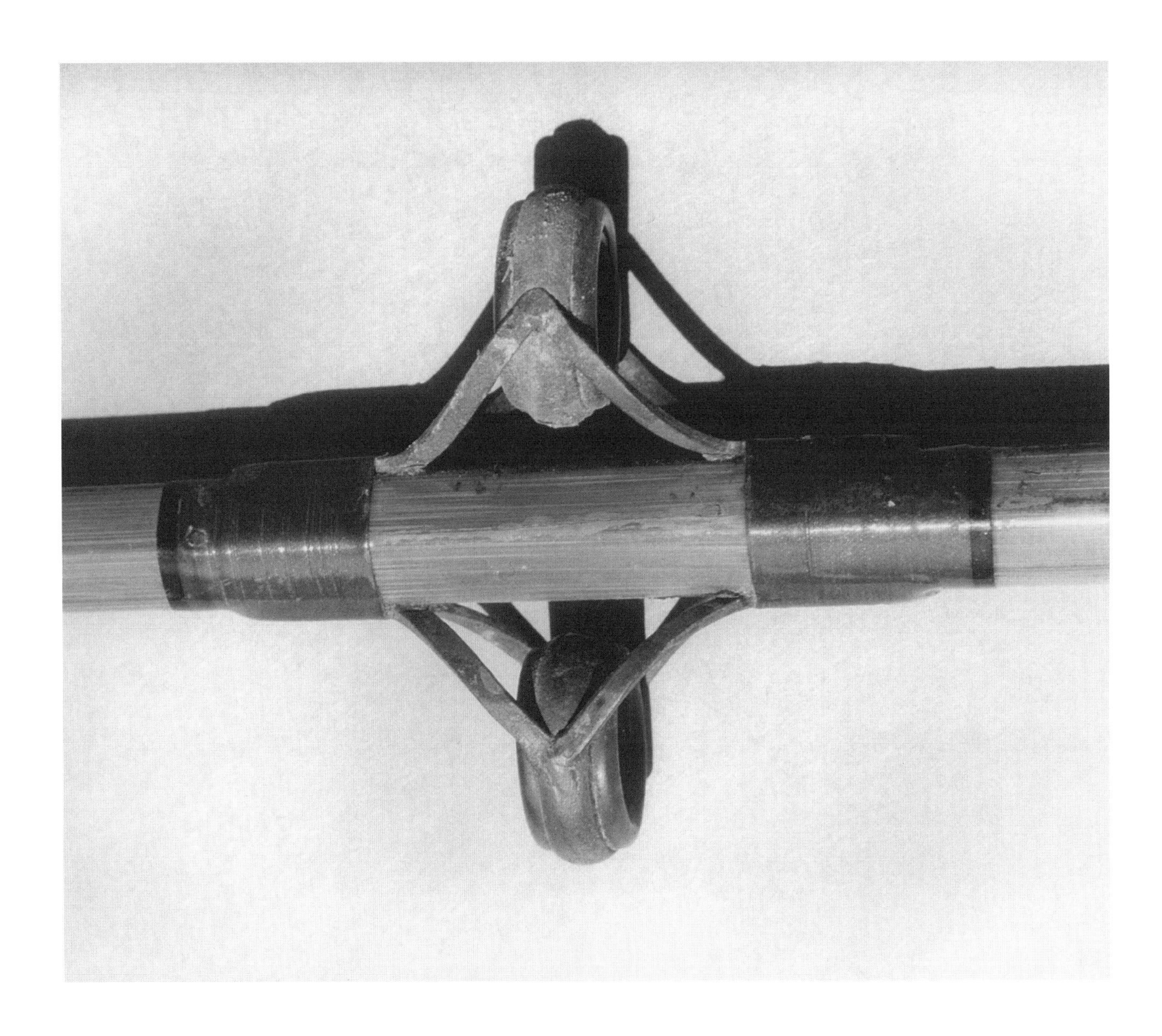

A good example of the double-sided (pair) guides found on the *West Coast* rod by H & I. The theory behind the pair guides is sound — under constant strain, bamboo will take a set. Before the days of stretchy monofilaments, our rigid braided lines put a heavy load on bamboo fibers. So, anglers alternated which side of the rod they used to provide even pressure on the blank. Rods of this nature were designed with either a revolving tip-top or "stirrup" type top through which the line could be threaded from either side.

Montague's *Monterey* was a low priced split bamboo ocean rod in the functional two-piece design. The Monterey shown above was built in Montaque City, Massachusetts circa 1949. This Monterey is equipped with hard chrome-plated guides on one side of the rod, an indicator of age. Earlier Monterey models (circa 1938) came with double-sided (pair) nickel silver guides and sold for as little as three dollars and fifty cents. For another buck an angler could have agate guides and tip-top in the *Somers Point* model.

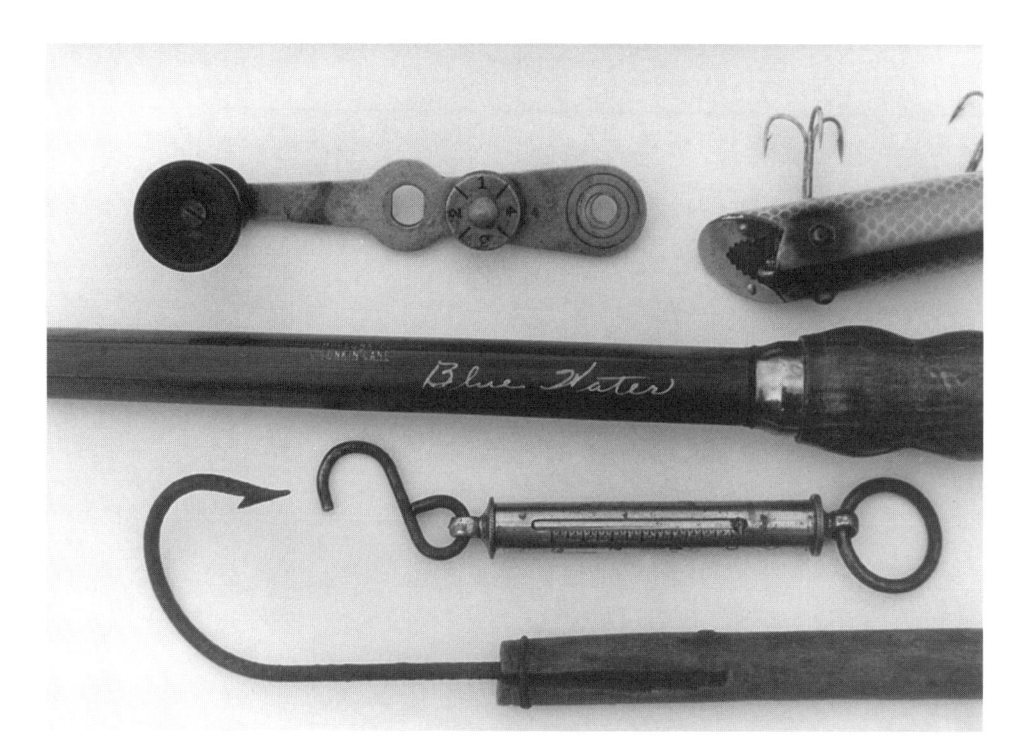

H & I *Blue Water* ocean rod constructed of dark, impregnated tonkin bamboo. Rods of this nature make interesting, inexpensive collectibles when displayed with angling paraphernalia such as nets, gaffs, scales and other nautical decor.

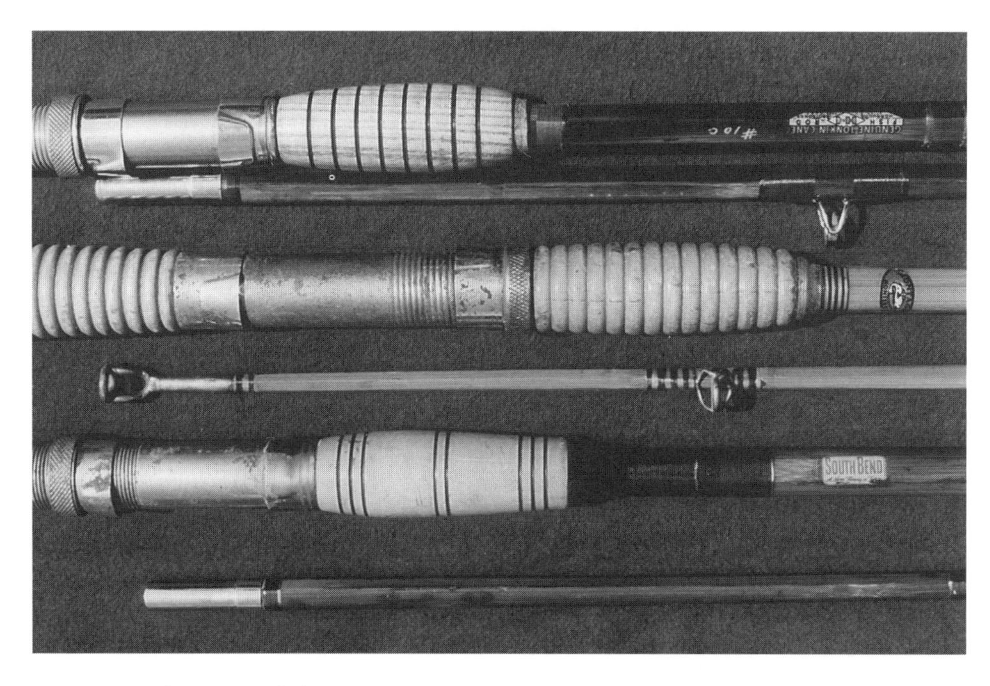

From **top** — a late model H & I #10, a stirrup-topped Montague, and a flamed South Bend. All are two-piece, six to seven foot bamboo boat rods circa 1950.

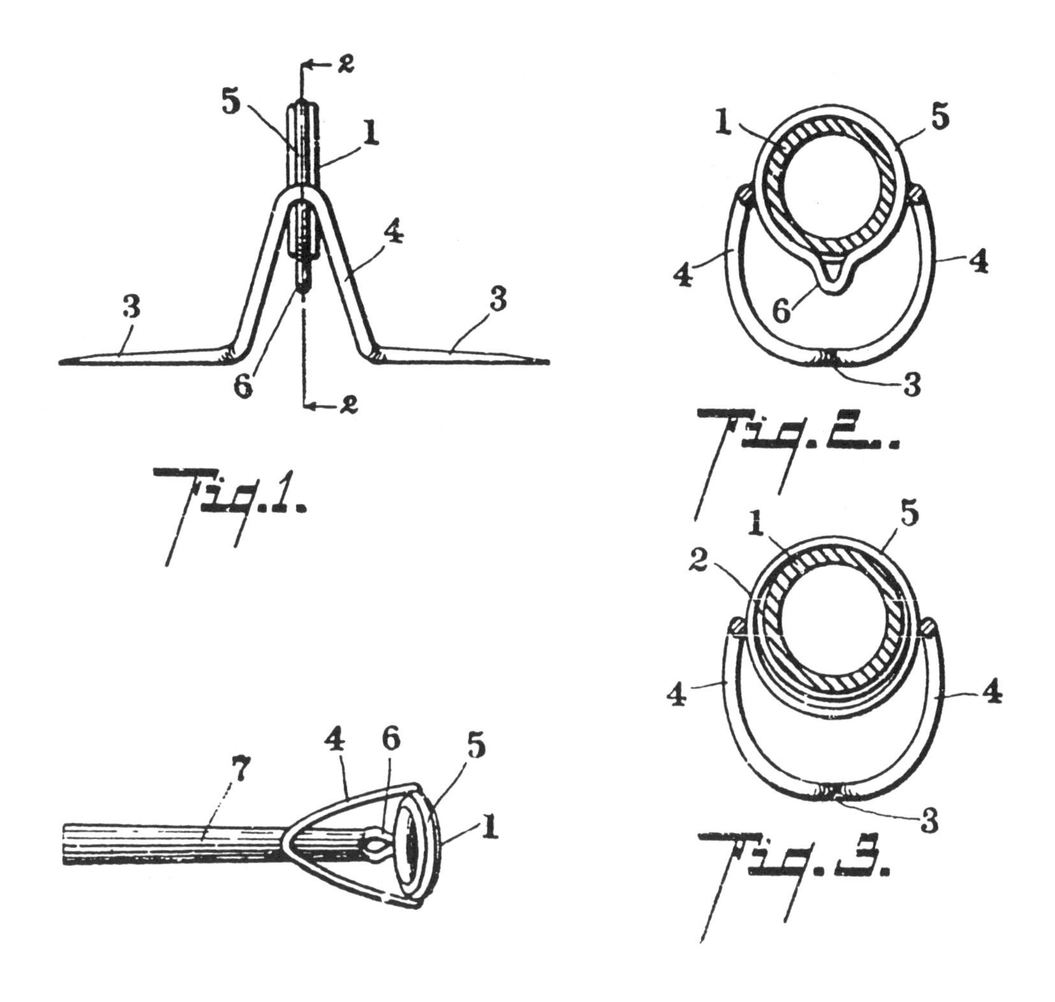

The William Shakespeare Jr. improved line guide patented May 24, 1910. This is a grandfather of many of the present day standing guides used for spinning and casting. It featured upward projecting yoke-like arms to support the eye and provided a distinct advantage in the manufacturing process because the support and securing ring could be joined together by hard solder or brazing without subjecting an expensive agate insert to intolerable heat. The agate or other material could be inserted later, in a separate step

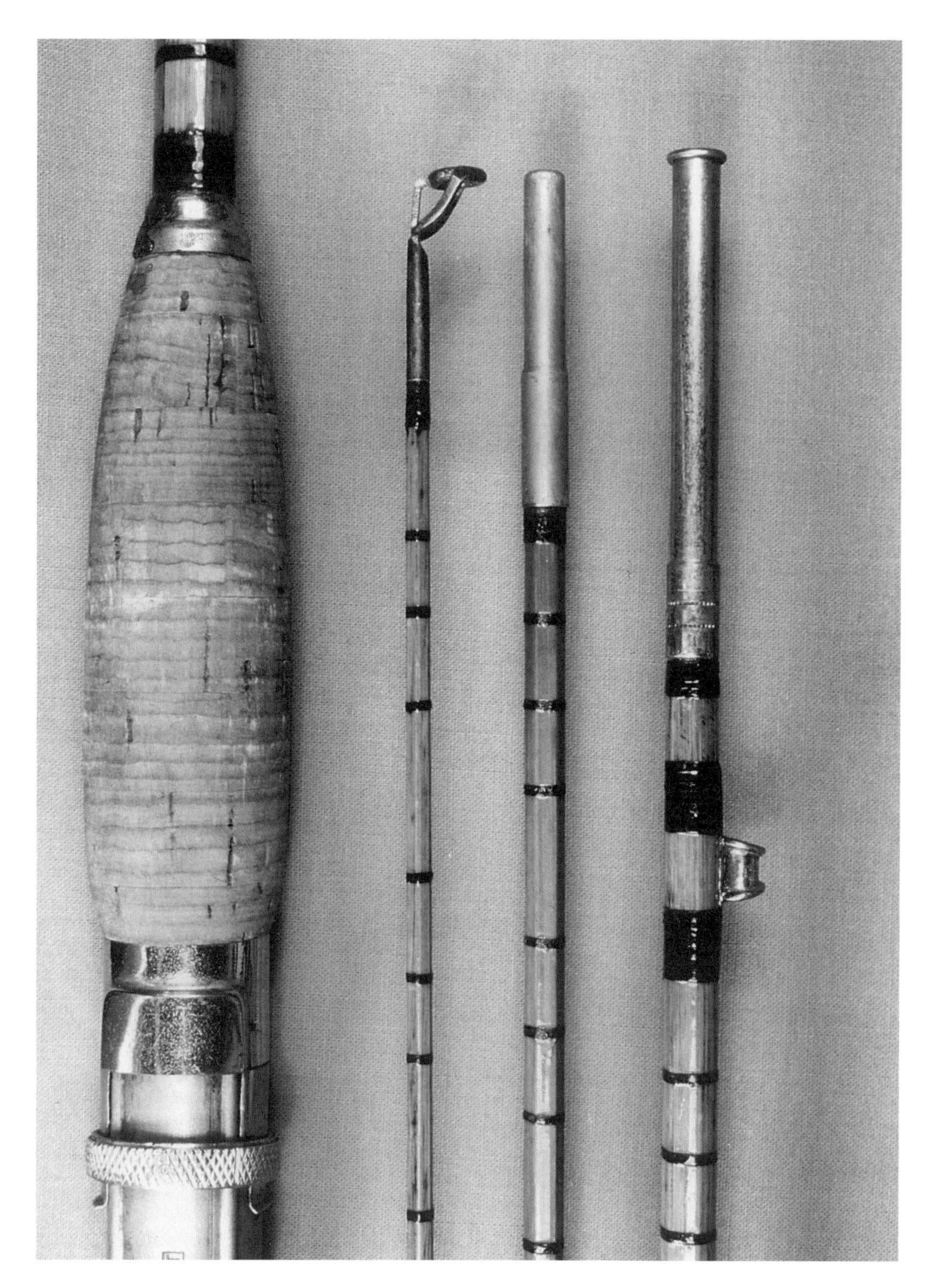

An unusual, but scary boat rod (circa 1920) that seems to have been restored using ferrules from several manufacturers (notice the two different styles and materials). The originality of the later-style cork grip comes into question when one considers the apparent age of the rod (compare the wide cork rings to the antiquated bell guides and full, intermediate windings).

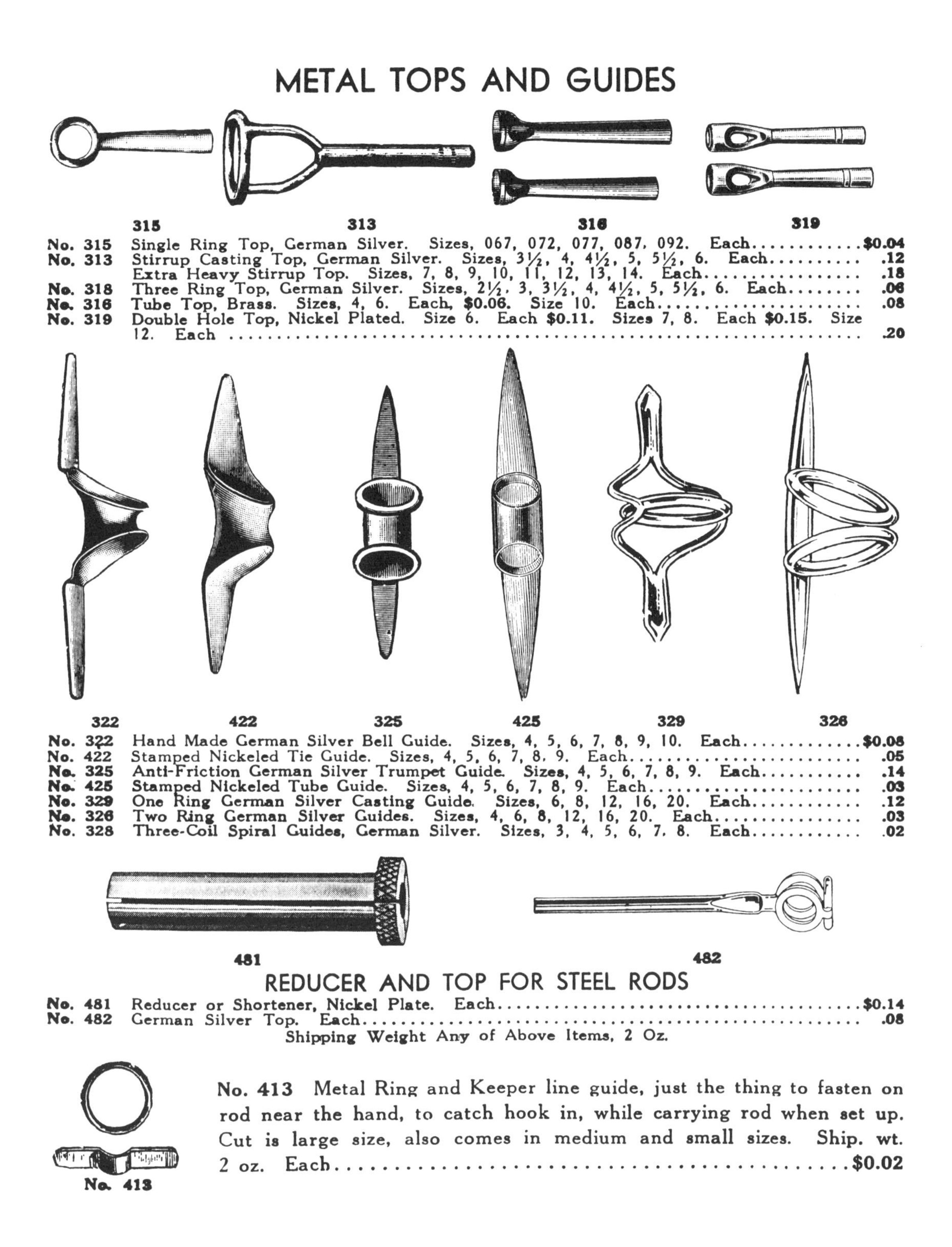

METAL TOPS AND GUIDES

No. 315 Single Ring Top, German Silver. Sizes, 067, 072, 077, 087, 092. Each........... $0.04
No. 313 Stirrup Casting Top, German Silver. Sizes, 3½, 4, 4½, 5, 5½, 6. Each.......... .12
Extra Heavy Stirrup Top. Sizes, 7, 8, 9, 10, 11, 12, 13, 14. Each................. .18
No. 318 Three Ring Top, German Silver. Sizes, 2½, 3, 3½, 4, 4½, 5, 5½, 6. Each........ .06
No. 316 Tube Top, Brass. Sizes, 4, 6. Each, $0.06. Size 10. Each..................... .08
No. 319 Double Hole Top, Nickel Plated. Size 6. Each $0.11. Sizes 7, 8. Each $0.15. Size 12. Each .... .20

No. 322 Hand Made German Silver Bell Guide. Sizes, 4, 5, 6, 7, 8, 9, 10. Each............. $0.08
No. 422 Stamped Nickeled Tie Guide. Sizes, 4, 5, 6, 7, 8, 9. Each....................... .05
No. 325 Anti-Friction German Silver Trumpet Guide. Sizes, 4, 5, 6, 7, 8, 9. Each........... .14
No. 425 Stamped Nickeled Tube Guide. Sizes, 4, 5, 6, 7, 8, 9. Each....................... .03
No. 329 One Ring German Silver Casting Guide. Sizes, 6, 8, 12, 16, 20. Each............ .12
No. 326 Two Ring German Silver Guides. Sizes, 4, 6, 8, 12, 16, 20. Each................ .03
No. 328 Three-Coil Spiral Guides, German Silver. Sizes, 3, 4, 5, 6, 7, 8. Each............ .02

REDUCER AND TOP FOR STEEL RODS

No. 481 Reducer or Shortener, Nickel Plate. Each.. $0.14
No. 482 German Silver Top. Each.. .08

Shipping Weight Any of Above Items, 2 Oz.

No. 413 Metal Ring and Keeper line guide, just the thing to fasten on rod near the hand, to catch hook in, while carrying rod when set up. Cut is large size, also comes in medium and small sizes. Ship. wt. 2 oz. Each.. $0.02

Rod builders and tackle tinkerers often ordered parts seen in catalog pages like the one pictured above (circa 1935). A good description of parts is evident

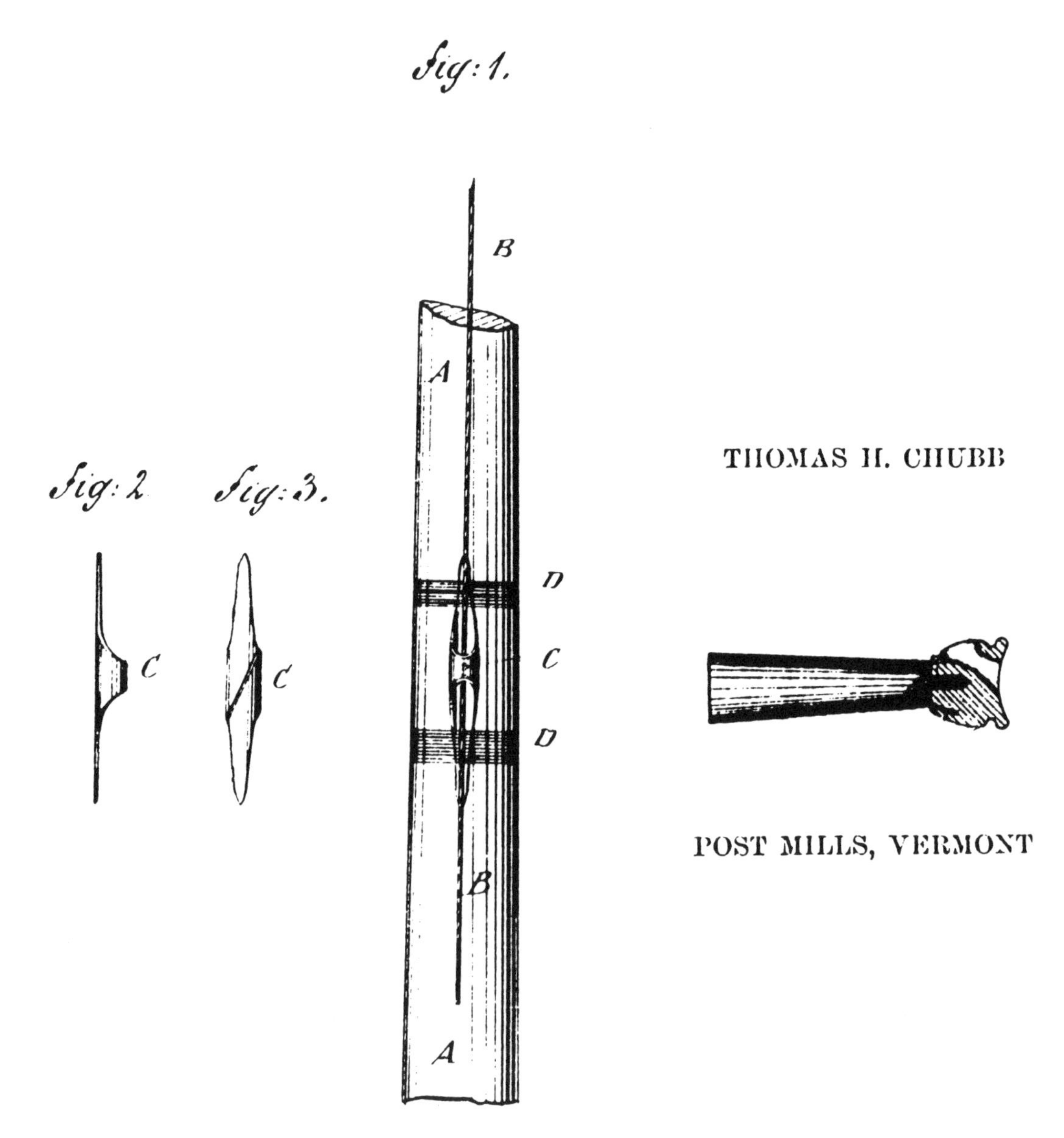

Two early Thomas Chubb patents were the "tunnel" or cylindrical tie-guide of 1882 and the "tube" top of 1883 with original drawings reproduced above. The tie-guide was ingeniously fabricated from one piece of sheet metal which was bent around a form to create the desired shape. Both of these basic designs were utilized on many boat and casting rods for fifty years.

Salt Water Rods

No. 64. A strongly built two piece split bamboo rod. Nickel plated mountings, welted shouldered ferrules, double cord wound grip, locking reel seat. Agatine first guide and tip top. Length 6 ft. Nicely wound with red silk. .... **Each $9.00**

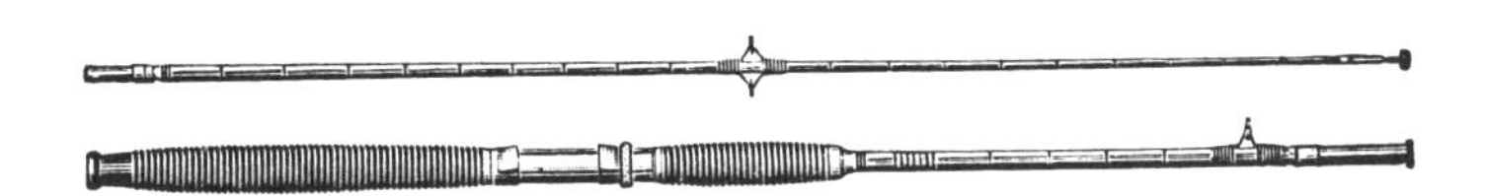

This two piece Boat Rod of exceptional value, is made of selected brown Tonkin cane with a hard wood double grip and rubber button. Nickel plated mountings, locking reel seat, all guides and top German silver. Wound with red and green silk and packed in a canvas partition bag. Length 5½ feet.

No. 431—Heavy (8 ferrule)...**Each $7.75**

No. 430—Medium (6 ferrule)...**Each 7.75**

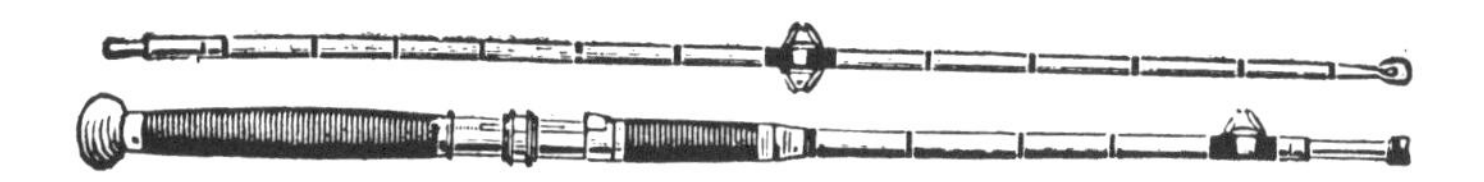

No. 805. Two pieces; split bamboo; nickel plated mountings; double wood grip and rubber button; locking reel seat; nickel double hole top; bell guides, wound with red silk. Put up in a partition bag. Length 5½ feet...**Each $6.00**

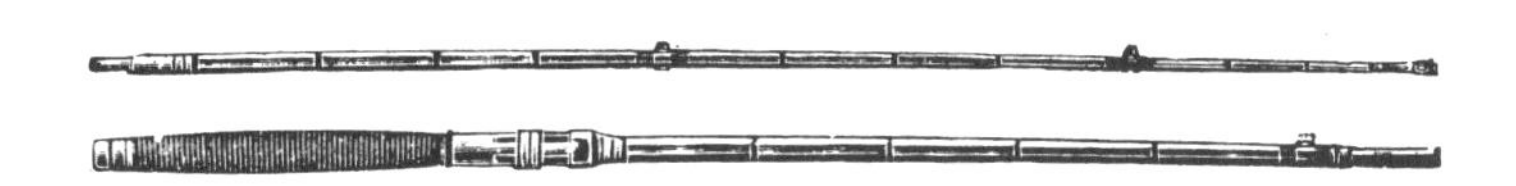

No. 42. Lightweight two piece Split Bamboo, 6 feet long, black enamel scored grip, 3 single bell guides wrapped with red silk and varnished, ¾ inch nickeled reel seat and nickeled butt cap ....**Each $3.00**

No. 62. Same description as above, but medium weight ⅞ inch reel seat, and all agatine guides and tip top ....**Each $5.00**

No. 82. Same description as No. 42 but heavy weight 1⅛ inch reel seat. **Each** **$5.50**

Page from a 1930 trade catalog depicting typical cane ocean rods of the time.

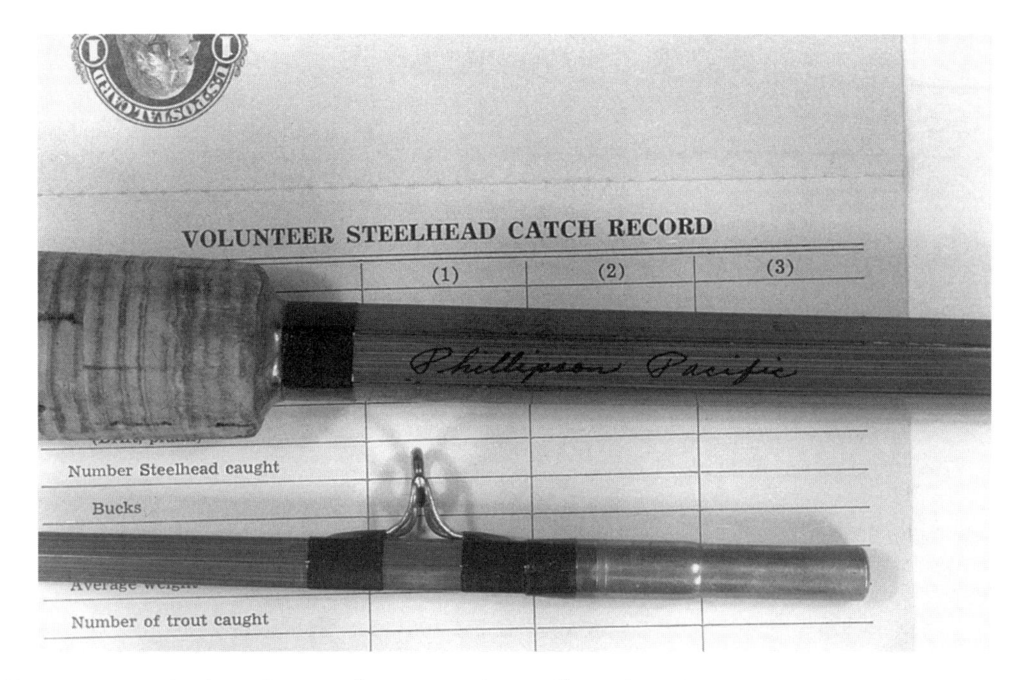

Phillipson *Pacific* bamboo salmon and steelhead rod measuring 9 feet in a two piece configuration. It has a chrome-plated screw-locking reel seat and fine, nickel-silver ferrules. Guides are the Mildrum type, non-reinforced and hard chrome plated. This is a terrific rod that is serviceable today.

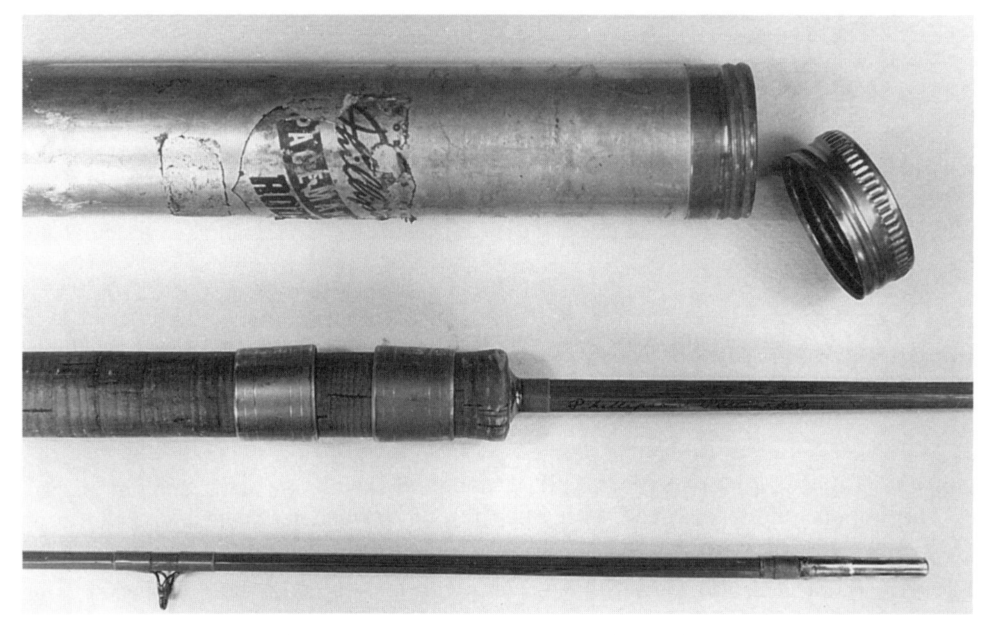

Phillipson *Pacemaker* bamboo spinning rod with the original aluminum tube. It is a parabolic 7 foot, 2 piece model. The guides are a blued, light wire spinning style — with a reinforcing brace on the largest one. Cork grip with sliding rings and blued, nickel-silver ferrules. The wrap colors are the same as found on Phillipson's Pacemaker fly rods (olive with yellow accents).

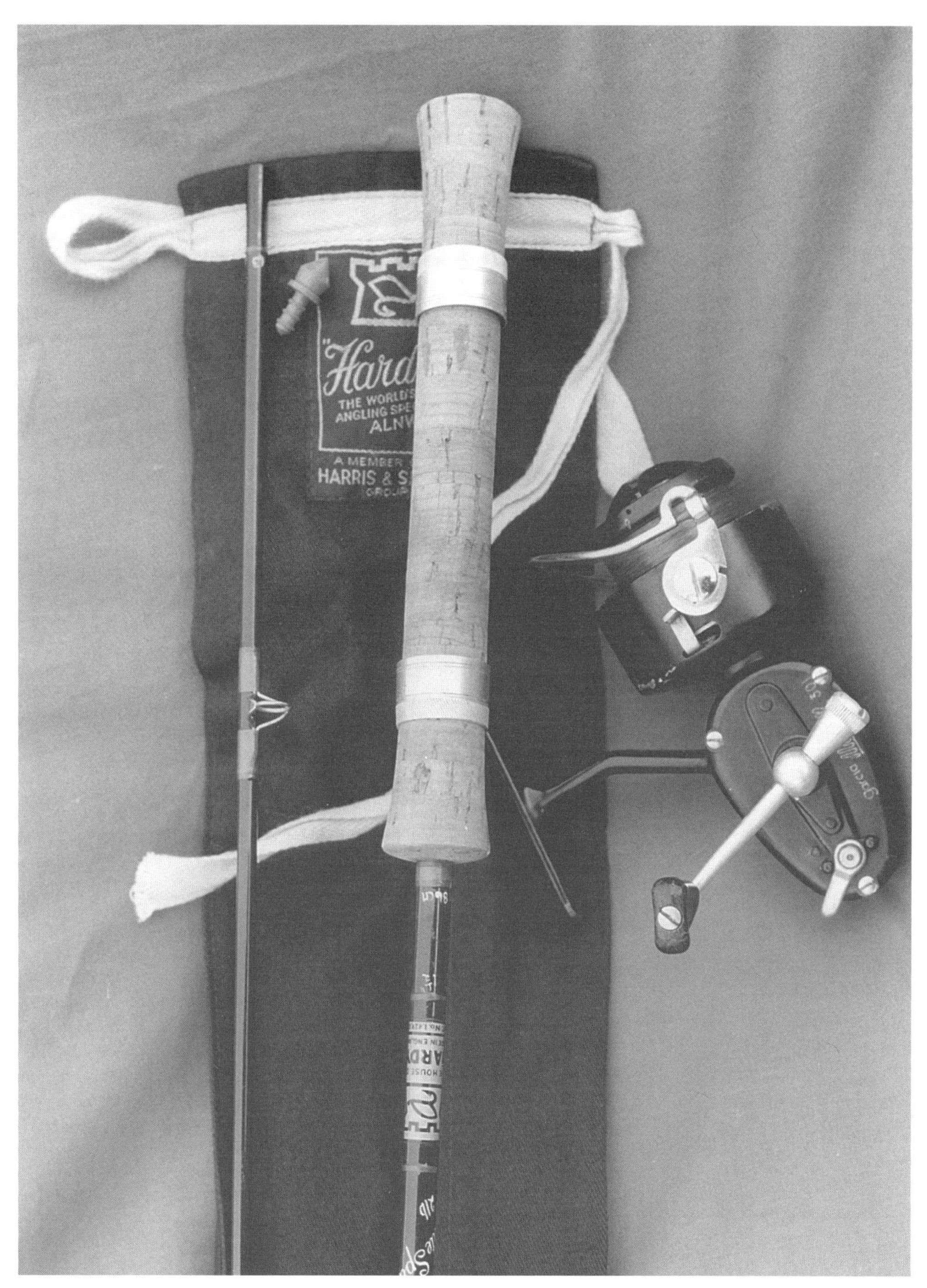

An outstanding Hardy *Fibalite* fiberglass spinning rod made in England around 1975. At a little over six feet, it is made especially for two pound test line and includes an agate tip-top. High grade ultra-light spinning rods, such as this, are the most eagerly collected fiberglass instruments — next to short glass fly rods.

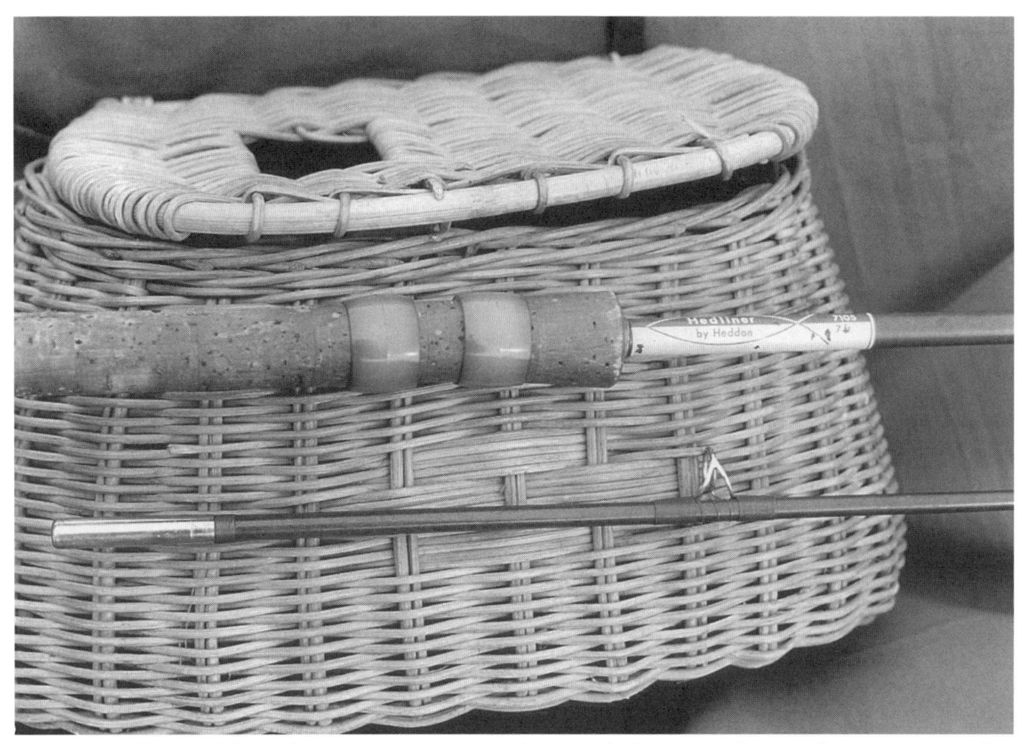

Heddon *Hedliner* fiberglass spinning rod (Model 7105) from the 1960s. This is a nostalgic, albeit low-end fishing collectible with good utility value.

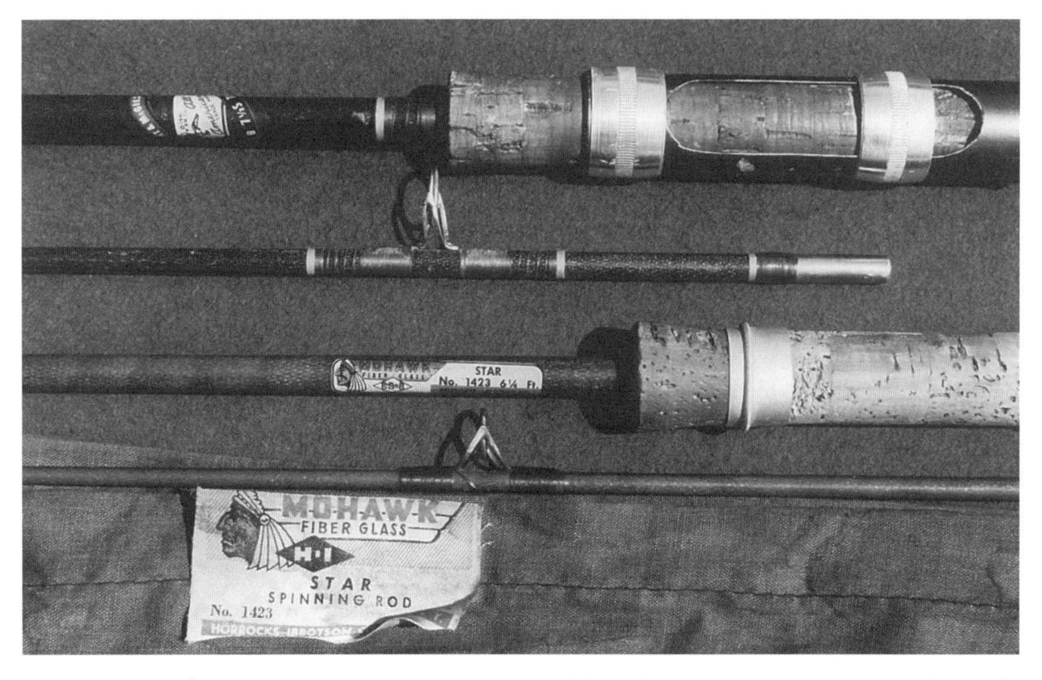

At **top** is Wright & McGill *All American* fiberglass spinning rod of 7 1/2 feet (Model B 7 1/2 S). The **bottom** rod is a 6 1/2 foot *Mohawk Star* (Model 1423) fiberglass spinning rod from H & I. Both were made circa 1955.

Condition Grading
and estimate of value

Due to the many subtleties and variations in the condition and fitness of collectible rods, it is difficult to provide an exact guideline for assigning condition grades such as *good* or *excellent*. Nonetheless, these grades are necessary in order to determine estimates of rod value. The entire process is certainly not precise and requires a bit of creativity and analysis on the part of the collector. The information and (often rather subjective) input from this book coupled with the readers own knowledge and experience should help to clarify the condition and pricing mystique.

The following represents **condition grade levels** used in the value guide of this book. Although these grade levels are the most common, they are not universally accepted by all fishing tackle collectors and dealers. Should this analysis by the author appear controversial to some, so be it. A wise man once said " . . . through the clash of differing opinions can be seen the light of truth" (or something to that effect!).

MINT CONDITION

The term *mint* is often exaggerated by zealous collectors and loosely used by dealers to describe a particularly nice rod. It is understandable when someone grades a rod as *excellent* and it is not. Erroneously assigning the mint or near mint grade is less forgivable when you consider the roots of the term *mint* (from coin collecting, meaning "new or uncirculated"). In rod collecting we are not quite so exacting as coin collectors and the mint designation might be stretched to describe a rod that looks perfect but has been cast on the lawn a few times. The mint rod may show signs of careful handling, yet the presence of slight imperfections such as almost indiscernible storage marks in the varnish may call for a designation of *near mint* or *excellent.*

For purposes of this book, the mint rod will always be accompanied by its original bag, case, tube etc. All original tags, labels, and decals should be pristine and included on the rod tube and bag.

The value guide groups together the rod grades of excellent to mint. Therefore, if the rod is truly mint, it could be valued higher than the listed amount. This can be looked at in another way — the excellent grade rod might be placed at a slightly lower than listed value. If the estimate of value is to establish a reasonable selling price, the slightly lower amount will help to effect a sale. Remember, appraising a collectible is one thing, but actually getting cold cash for it is another!

EXCELLENT CONDITION (EX)

The grade of *excellent* may be the most controversial evaluation term used in the hobby of rod collecting. Many questions surround this **top grade**. Remember, if we reserve the mint grade for essentially "unfished" rods then *excellent* is the highest grade that can be assigned to a second hand rod — and should not be taken lightly!

As a general rule, a rod in excellent condition will be just as it came from the manufacturer except it will have been fished a few times. If it is a varnished bamboo rod, the finish will be fine and sound — not soft or tacky. The guide "wraps" and intermediates are not frayed or cracked. All ferrules and hardware should be tight, clean and functional. Look at the rod closely. Are there any broken or missing sections, are the guides worn or bent, has the rod been altered in any way?

Should a professionally restored or refinished rod be called an "excellent condition" rod? I think not! The term *mint restored* is commonly used by collector/dealers and would seem more appropriate. If it is a question of value, the professionally restored rod could be placed at the excellent price level (or lower if structural restoration has taken place). The quality of the refinish must be scrutinized to determine whether the rod need be lowered to the good-vg or poor-fair value level. Should a rod be "restored" by the local handy man, beware! The well-meaning but unskilled handy man has accounted for the destruction and devaluation of many fine rods.

In most cases, one should expect that a rod graded and priced at the excellent level will include the original bag, and storage tube. If these items are not included and known to have been a part of the original outfit, the rod should be dropped to a lower price level.

Broken or fractured mid or butt sections are surely not acceptable at this high level of condition, but what about a tip that is broken only one inch down from the top? What about two inches — where do we draw the line? Certainly, a rod equipped with only one tip cannot be assigned to this condition level with a break of any kind. If a two-tip rod is genuinely excellent in every way and the extra tip is slightly short, the rod could still be placed at the excellent level. We must look to the length and action of the rod to determine how short is too short. A light, fast 7 1/2 foot bamboo fly rod may not function at all well with two inches broken off at the tip. However a soft, parabolic 9 foot fly rod might be acceptable with an inch or two broken-off one tip. Appraising a rod exhibiting any defect is tricky business. I, like many other conservative collectors, would deduct substantially from the excellent price level for even the slightest tip-break.

Summary • **Excellent Condition**

(1) Fine, original finish

(2) No missing sections or components

(3) No breaks, fractures, dirt or wear

(4) Shows evidence of only minimal use

(4) Original bag and case with tags and labels

VERY GOOD CONDITION (VG)

The greatest misconception in rod evaluation by the general antique dealer or collector not familiar with fishing rods is the notion that any old rod is in "very good" condition. This makes sense because the casual observer, fringe hobbyist or beginner is likely to disregard the utility of the rod in favor of its "antique" appearance. If you are not an angler, it is hard to distinguish between a decent, complete, usable rod and a "decorator piece" that would fall apart on the first cast.

A rod in *very good condition* should be completely sound and not display evidence of hard use or abuse. Most collectors would expect the rod to be accompanied by its original bag and tube (if the rod originally came enclosed in a tube).

A short extra tip might be acceptable at this condition level, as would a repairable set in a mid or tip section. One neatly replaced guide, or a minor chipping of the cork grip are other examples of tolerable flaws at this level.

Evaluate the entire rod as a whole. A complete, straight, original rod with all the correct accompaniments and an extra tip might have one tip that is 2" short, one replaced guide, a touch-up of the varnish in two spots and still be considered *very good* for valuation purposes. Add a loose ferrule and frayed or dried-out guide wraps — and the rod's condition is lowered to *good* or probably *fair* depending upon the severity of the maladies.

On occasion a rod is found in very good or even excellent condition yet it is missing the original bag and/or case. The rod can then be valued at the appropriate level with a reasonable deduction to account for the missing accompaniments. A slight reduction in value can result from a missing screw-cap or top to the rod's tube. Remember, no matter what the condition, a rod is imminently more collectible when enclosed in its original bag and tube (case).

Bear in mind, that the prices stated in the value guide reflect averages and cannot possible take into account the vast combination of variable and flaws seen on each rod you are evaluating. For example: If the rod you are evaluating seems to fall between condition levels, price it between condition levels or develop your own sliding scale derived from values stated herein. Try to be creative yet accurate at the same time!

Summary • **Very Good Condition**

(1) Original rod finish with few flaws

(2) Grip, ferrules and reel seat show average, moderate use

(3) No missing or altered components (exceptions noted above)

(4) Some minor wear to guides and wraps acceptable

(5) Rod is complete with original bag and case

(6) Rod was generally well maintained and is fully functional

GOOD CONDITION

A rod in good condition is essentially the same as one in very good condition — it is "fishable" with a few more maladies or slightly more wear and tear. It should be mostly original and authentic with enough repair or maintenance work upon it to be noticeable without being obnoxious! A repair wrap to a small hook dig, a couple of rewrapped or touched-up guides, a fine over-varnish, heavily soiled cork, or a short tip (in a two-tip rod) may be acceptable at this value level. Whether these maladies are all acceptable in one rod is the question which must be answered. Again, the rod's attributes and accompaniments must be considered as a whole. Often it is a few positive features which keep the rod from sinking into the poor-fair category. If you have a good feeling about a rod, it is complete and authentic, but has one too many flaws — price it between the poor-fair and good-vg level.

FAIR CONDITION

A common characteristic of a *fair* rod is that it has either been poorly refinished or it needs some degree of restoration/refinishing work. Cracked, missing, altered, or inappropriately replaced components and rod sections often make up the physiology of a rod in fair condition. We are talking more about damage here, rather than use and wear. Usually the original bag and tube are missing or replaced.

The difference between the fair rod and the poor rod is that the fair rod needs much less work to restore it to true fishing condition. The less work needed, the more the value can be pushed toward the good-vg level. It's that simple.

Some fair condition rods are better-off left alone. A well-used, damaged but authentic antique rod can still be quite charming and alluring as is. And it won't cost a fortune to procure it!

POOR CONDITION

The rod in this category needs a complete restoration, which might include the construction of new rod sections. A scarce or highly sought-after collectible rod may be worth saving — so its *poor value* may be substantial compared to a more common rod.

Collectors and hobbyists do look for lower condition rods to restore as projects. Most of these people are not rod makers nor are they skilled professionals. Their work is more apt to devalue rather than enhance the value of a rod. However, with a bit of tinkering and a measure of patience, some poor condition rods can be adequately restored by the amateur angler for his or her own use on the water.

A great example of a fly rod in poor condition. Maladies include a short tip, missing tip, no bag or case, damaged cork, replaced hardware, rusted guides, and a loose ferrule.

Fishing Rod Value Guide

- Rods are split bamboo unless otherwise noted
- (3/2) describes a three piece rod with two tips

ABBEY & IMBRIE

ABBEY & IMBRIE	poor-fair	good-vg	ex-mint
“Best” Calcutta fly rod 10 1/2’ (3/2) c.1900	60	175	325
“A & I” trout fly rod 8’ (3/2) form case c.1910	50	165	300
“Centennial” fly rod 9 1/2’ (3/2) c.1917	45	135	235
“A & I” fly rod by Heddon 9’ (3/2) c.1930	40	110	200
“Featherweight” fly rod 8’ (3/2) c.1930	45	120	215
“A& I” antique trout fly rod 9 1/2” sheet cork grip	30	75	165
“A & I” antique trout rod 11 1/2’ ring guides c.1890	40	145	260
“A & I” antique greenheart wood fly rod 10’ (3/1)	40	135	210
Lancewood bicycle rod (4/2) with canvas cover c.1898	40	125	200
“A & I” steel pack rod by Horton 4 1/2’ (5/1) c.1915	12	30	60

ABERCROMBY & FITCH

ABERCROMBY & FITCH	poor-fair	good-vg	ex-mint
“DF Special” fly rod by Phillipson 8 1/2’ (3/2)	45	175	300
“Firehole” fly rod by Phillipson 7 1/2’ (2/2)	75	275	525
“Firehole” fly rod 8’ (2/2) c.1968	50	175	310
“Firehole” fly rod 8 1/2’ (3/2)	40	125	235
“Yellowstone” fly rod 8 1/2 - 9’ (3/2)	40	110	200
“Yellowstone Special” by Edwards 8’ (3/2)	55	185	325
“Triton” fly rod by Edwards 8’ (3/2)	65	235	400
“Favorite” fly rod by Edwards 7 1/2’ (2/2)	75	270	475
“A & F No. 2” fly rod by Milward 7 1/2’ (2/2)	60	195	375
“Catskill” fly rod 9’ (3/2) c.1910 in form case	50	130	225
“A & F” salmon fly rod by Pezon et Michel 9’ (3/1)	40	100	200
“Midget” spin rod by Pezon et Michel 5 1/2’ (2/1)	55	155	275
A & F ultra-light spinning rod 5’ (2/1)	55	140	245
A & F boat rod by Montague 8 1/2’ (3/2)	15	35	75
A & F “Banty” fiberglass fly rod 4’4” (2/1) c.1965	10	40	90

A & F “Featherweight” fiberglass fly rod 7’ (2/1)	8	30	60
A & F “Featherweight” fiberglass fly rod 8 1/2’ (2/1)	6	20	40
A & F “Banty” fiberglass spinning rod 4’4” (2/1)	8	30	70
A & F “Favorite” fiberglass ultra-lite spinning rod	5	18	40
Payne fly rods sold by A&F (see Payne Rod Co.)	x	x	x

ALLCOCK (England)	poor-fair	good-vg	ex-mint
“Marvel” trout fly rod 8’ (2/1) spiked ferrules	65	165	275
Dry fly salmon rod 10’ (2/2)	40	110	200
Heavy trout fly rod 9’ (2/1)	35	85	165
“Allcock’s Sapper” salmon fly rod 10’ (3/1)	35	90	165
“Light Caster” spinning rod 7’ (2/1)	20	65	125

BARNEY & BERRY	poor-fair	good-vg	ex-mint
Trout fly rod by E.W. Edwards 9’ (3/2)	50	140	240
Trout fly rod by E.W. Edwards 8 1/2’ (3/2)	65	165	265

L.L. BEAN	poor-fair	good-vg	ex-mint
Trout fly rod by Edwards 7 1/2’ (2/2) c.1930	100	290	475
Trout fly rod by Phillipson 8 1/2’ (3/2) c.1955	60	165	295
Salmon fly rod by Montague 9 1/2’ (3/2)	35	80	165
Solid steel octagonal baitcasting rods c.1938	4	12	30
Fiberglass fly rod 8’ (2/1) “Phillipson Epoxite” c.1965	12	35	75
Fiberglass fly rod 8’ (2/1) brown c.1955	10	25	50
Fiberglass spinning rod 6 1/2’ (2/1) c.1958	4	12	25
Fiberglass casting rod 5 1/2’ (1 pc) c.1954	3	10	20
Fiberglass trolling rod 6 1/2’ (w/handle) c.1955	3	9	18

BRISTOL - HORTON MFG.	poor-fair	good-vg	ex-mint
Model F-3 fly rod by Edwards 8 1/2’ (3/2)	50	155	265
Model F-5 fly rod by Edwards 9’ (3/2)	50	150	235
Model F-7 fly rod by Edwards 8 1/2’ (3/2)	55	170	295
Model F-12 fly rod by Edwards 8 1/2’ (3/2)	60	175	310

Model F-18 fly rod by Edwards 8 1/2 ‘ (3/2)	65	180	325
Model F-18 fly rod by Edwards 9’ (3/2)	50	145	260
Antique steel fly rod 8 1/2’ (3/1) c.1905	9	28	50
Antique telescoping steel fly rod 10’ (maple handle)	10	30	55
Telescoping steel bass rod 9 1/2’ (maple handle) c.1905	10	30	55
Steel fly-pack rod (4 pc. 2 tips) leather case	15	40	85
#16 tubular steel fly rod 9’ (3/1) c.1927	6	18	35
#25 tubular steel fly rod 8’ (2/1) c.1930	6	18	35
#33 steel bait casting rod 6’ (3/1) c.1925	5	16	28
Tubular steel casting rod 5 - 5 1/2’ 1 pc.	5	16	28
Tubular steel fly/bait rod with reversible handle c.1920	5	16	28
Telescoping tubular steel spinning rod 8’	5	15	25
Antique steel boat rod 5’ (4/1) agate tip-top	7	20	40
Fiberglass baitcasting rod 6 1/2’ (1 pc.) c.1955	3	8	15

THOMAS CHUBB	poor-fair	good-vg	ex-mint
C. 1890 antique lancewood fly rod 10’	45	95	195
C. 1880 antique ash boat rod 8’	40	85	165
C. 1890 calcutta fly rod 10’ (3/2) rattan grip & flip guides	70	170	325
“Henshall” bait rod 8’ 9” (3/2) with patented funnel top	50	95	195
“Union League” lancewood fly rod 10 1/2’ (4/2)	40	125	225
“Union League” split bamboo fly rod 10 1/2’ (4/2)	50	145	275
“Little Giant” calcutta casting rod 7 1/2’ (2/2) c. 1890	50	110	225
“Little Giant” greenheart bass casting rod 7 1/2’ (2/2)	40	90	190
Chubb antique wood salmon rod 15’ with funnel top	40	95	200
Thomas Chubb wood valise (7 pc.) rod 10’ c.1895	40	85	175

CONROY & BISSETT	poor-fair	good-vg	ex-mint
Antique Calcutta trout fly rod 12’ (3/2) c.1885	135	250	475
“Conroy” Calcutta trout fly rod by Varney 8 1/2’ (3/2)	145	325	600

CONSTABLE (England)	poor-fair	good-vg	ex-mint
“Empress” fly rod 8’ (2/2) staggered ferrule	50	140	295

"Wallop Brook" fly rod 6' 9" (2/1) SF	40	125	235
"Wallop Brook" fly rod 7 1/2' (2/1) SF	40	120	225
"Wallop Brook fly rod 8' (2/1) staggered ferrule	40	120	210
"Dart" fly rod 5' 9" (2/2)	60	170	325
"R.H. Woods Classic" fly rod 6'9" (2/2)	65	175	350
"R.H. Woods Eighty Two" fly rod 8'2" (2/2)	50	150	300
"Sceptre Glass" fiberglass fly rod 9' (2/1) c.1970	20	40	85

CORTLAND	poor-fair	good-vg	ex-mint
444 LTD fly rod by Farlow 8' (2/1)	40	110	195
444 LTD fly rod by Farlow 8' (2/2)	60	165	275
444 LTD fly rod by Farlow 7 1/2' (2/2)	75	190	335
444 LTD fly rod by Farlow 7' (2/2)	80	195	365
444 LTD fly rod by Farlow 6 1/2' (2/2)	85	200	375
"Leon Chandler" fiberglass fly rod 8 1/2' (2/1)	9	22	40

CROSS ROD CO.	poor-fair	good-vg	ex-mint
Trout fly rod made in Lynn, Mass. 7 1/2' (3/2)	120	295	495
"Cross" Deluxe trout fly rod 7' (2/2)	140	370	625
Trout fly rod made in Lynn, Mass. 9' (3/2)	50	135	250
"Forsyth" trout fly rod 8 1/2' (3/2)	55	140	275
"Double Built" trout fly rod 9' (3/2) c.1920	60	140	275
"Single Built" trout fly rod 9' (3/2)	45	120	225
Cross light salmon fly rod 9 1/2' (3/2)	35	90	195
Early Cross salmon fly rod 10' (3/2) c.1915	45	115	210
Cross two handed salmon rod 12' (3/2)	35	80	185
Cross "Model 166" salmon fly rod 9' (3/2) c.1920	40	85	200
Cross 7' boat rod with turned wood handle	12	30	65
Cross casting rod 6' (1 pc.) agate guides c. 1910	20	50	95

DAME STODDARD & CO.	poor-fair	good-vg	ex-mint
Trout fly rod 8 1/2' (3/2)	50	135	250
Trout fly rod by F.E. Thomas 9 1/2' (3/2)	65	170	300

Antique lancewood fly rod 9 1/2' (3/2) rattan grip	40	125	200
"Henshall" greenheart casting rod 8' 3" (2/1) c.1880	35	95	160

DEVINE ROD CO.

	poor-fair	good-vg	ex-mint
"The Devine Rod" early fly rod 9' (3/2)	65	195	350
"Fairy" fly rod 7 1/2' (3/2) sold by Folsom c. 1930	150	375	725
Divine Calcutta trout fly rod 8' (3/2) c.1900	75	195	400
Fred Devine fly rod 8' (3/2) c.1925	85	210	450
Fred Devine fly rod 8 1/2' (3/2)	65	150	300
Fred Devine "Browntone" fly rod 9' (3/2)	75	175	350
"Gloriwest" fly rod by Divine 9' (3/2)	50	145	275
Antique greenheart wood fly rod 10 1/2 ' (3/2)	40	80	145
Antique wood bass rod 10' (3/2) form case	30	75	125
Devine baitcasting rod 6 1/2' (3/2) c.1915	40	85	175

DICKERSON

	poor-fair	good-vg	ex-mint
Model #9618 heavy trout fly rod 9 1/2' (3/2)	300	900	1700
Model #9018 heavy trout fly rod 9' (3/2)	300	900	1700
Model #8016 trout fly rod 8' (3/2)	500	1500	2500
Model #8615 trout fly rod 8 1/2' (2/2)	450	1200	2000
Model #8616 heavy trout fly rod 8 1/2' (3/2)	400	1100	1800
Model #8014 trout fly rod 8' (2/2)	550	1500	2600
Model #8013 trout fly rod 8' (2/2)	650	1700	3000
Model #7013 trout fly rod 7' (2/2)	900	2400	4800
Model #7615 trout fly rod 7 1/2' (2/2)	850	2000	4000
Model #7613 trout fly rod 7 1/2' (2/2)	900	2200	4200

SEWELL DUNTON

	poor-fair	good-vg	ex-mint
"Model 152" trout fly rod 7' (2/2)	50	165	325
"Model 158" trout fly rod 8' (2/2)	40	135	275
"Dunton & Sons" fly rod 7 1/2' (2/2)	45	145	285
"Angler's Choice" fly rod 8 1/2' (3/2)	30	95	195
"Standard" trout fly rod 8' (3/2)	25	75	185

“Model 107” trout fly rod 8’ (3/2)	30	85	195
“Dunton” light salmon fly rod 9’ (3/2)	20	60	160

EDWARDS	poor-fair	good-vg	ex-mint
E.W. Edwards “Special” fly rod 9’ (3/2) c. 1915	115	275	500
E.W. Edwards salmon fly rod 10 1/2’ (3/2)	75	175	350
E.W. Edwards “Perfection” fly rod 9’ (3/2)	110	265	495
E.W. Edwards “Mt. Carmel” fly rod 8’ (3/2)	125	295	600
E.W. Edwards “Deluxe” fly rod 7’ (2/2) c. 1920	250	600	1200
E.W. E. & Sons fly rod 8 1/2’ (3/2) c.1927	115	285	525
E.W. E. & Sons “Ed. Special” fly 8 1/2’ (3/2) c.1932	115	285	500
E.W. E. & Sons “Ed. Special” fly rod 9’ (3/2) c.1930	105	260	485
Edwards “Bristol” boat rod 6 1/2’ (1 pc.)	40	90	175
Bill Edwards “Quad” #34 fly rod 8’ (3/2)	175	400	800
Bill Edwards “Quad” #35 fly rod 8 1/2 (3/2)	150	400	700
Bill Edwards “Quad” #40 fly rod 7’ (2/2)	300	700	1200
Bill Edwards “Quad” #41 fly rod 7’ (2/2)	300	700	1200
Bill Edwards “Quad Deluxe” fly rod 7 1/2’ (3/2)	300	700	1200
Bill Edwards “Quad” #43 fly rod 8’ (2/2)	200	450	900
Bill Edwards “Quad” #53 fly rod 8 1/2’ (3/2)	175	400	850
Bill Edwards “Quad” #56 fly rod 9’ (3/2)	135	275	550
Bill Edwards “Quad” #67 salmon fly rod 10’ (3/2)	100	200	400
Edwards “Quad” spinning rod 7’ (2/1)	65	195	375
Edwards “Special Luxor” spin rod 7’ (2/1)	65	195	375
Edwards “Quad” bait casting rod 5 1/2’ (2/1)	70	200	395
Edwards Model #40 “Deluxe” spinning rod 7’ (2/1)	50	125	235
Gene Edwards “Deluxe” spinning rod 7’ (2/1)	50	125	235
Gene Edwards “Deluxe” fly rod 9’ (3/2)	100	235	375
Gene Edwards “Deluxe” fly rod 8 1/2’ (3/2)	135	325	575
Gene Edwards “Deluxe” baitcasting rod 5’ (2/1)	60	165	295
Gene Edwards light trout fly rod 7’ (2/2)	200	400	850
Gene Edwards fiberglass salmon rod 9 1/2’ (3/2)	20	40	75

FARLOW (England & Scotland)	poor-fair	good-vg	ex-mint
“Ultimate” trout fly rod 5’ 10” (1 piece design)	60	185	365
“Lee Wulff” midge 6’ (2/2) sold by Norm Thompson	65	215	400
“Lee Wulff” fly rod 8’ (2/1) impregnated (Scotland)	50	160	300
“Farlow” light trout fly rod 7’ 3” (2/2)	75	225	425
“Farlow” trout fly rod 7’ 9” (2/1) staggered ferrule	50	160	300
“Featherweight” trout fly rod 8’ (2/1) impregnated	50	160	300
“Wilson International” trout fly rod 8’ 9” (2/2)	65	190	375
C. 1900 antique fly rod Calcutta bamboo 10’ (3/2)	40	125	250
“Morgan” two-handed salmon fly rod 14’ (3/2)	40	120	225
Antique trout fly rod 9’ (3/1) with screw-lock ferrules	30	80	150
Antique greenheart wood fly rod 10’ (3/2)	35	95	195

FENWICK	poor-fair	good-vg	ex-mint
Fiberglass fly rods c.1965-1975	10	35	70
Fiberglass casting rods c.1965-1975	7	18	35
Fiberglass spinning rods c.1965-1975	8	22	45
Fiberglass saltwater rods c.1965-1975	8	22	45

FOLSOM ARMS CO.	poor-fair	good-vg	ex-mint
Model #1510 trout fly rod by Heddon 8 1/2’ (3/2)	60	150	300
Model #1515 trout fly rod by Heddon 9’ (3/2)	55	120	240
Model #1515 trout fly rod by Heddon 8 1/2’ (3/2)	65	165	325
Model #1525 trout fly rod by Heddon 8’ (3/2)	75	185	350
“The Amawalk” trout fly rod 8 1/2’ (3/2) c. 1930	50	120	215
Trout fly rod by Hardy (England) 8’ (3/2) c.1935	60	140	280
Folsom salmon fly rod w/ fighting butt 9 1/2’ (3/2)	45	100	195
Early fly & casting rod 9 1/2’ (3/2) reversible handle	20	75	145
“The Hawley” casting rod 5’ (2/1) English made1932	30	65	95
“The Nokabout” greenheart casting rod 6’ (4/1)	25	45	85
Pack rod 6 1/2’ (7/2) with reversible handle c.1925	25	60	120
Saltwater boat rods 6 - 6 1/2’ (2/1) c.1930	15	35	75
Deep sea rods greenheart wood 5 - 6’ (3/1)	15	35	75

"Capitol" solid steel casting rod 5' (1pc.)	4	9	18
"Broadway" tubular steel casting rod 5 1/2' (4/1)	6	12	22
"Broadway" steel fly rod 7' (2/1) "bamboo" painted	9	18	38
"VIM" steel rods 6 - 9' (3/1) 3-ring top c.1930	3	8	15

FOSTERS (England)	poor-fair	good-vg	ex-mint
"The Wisp" trout fly rod 6' (2/1)	60	165	300
"Champion" trout fly rod 8' (2/1)	45	120	200
Trout fly rod 8 1/2' (3/1)	30	85	160
Heavy trout fly rod 8 1/2' (2/1)	25	70	140
Steel center antique fly rods 10' c.1900	40	110	195

GARCIA	poor-fair	good-vg	ex-mint
Model 2731 fiberglass fly rod c.1965	4	14	30
Model 2701-2704 fiberglass spinning rods c.1965	4	10	25
Early "Conolon" fiberglass rods	4	9	22
Ocean & baitcasting fiberglass rods c.1970	3	9	20

EVERETT GARRISON	poor-fair	good-vg	ex-mint
Model 204 trout fly rod 7 1/2' (2/2)	N/A	5000	9000
Model 206 trout fly rod 7 1/2' (2/2)	N/A	4800	8500
Model 209 trout fly rod 8' (2/2)	N/A	3700	8000
Model 212 trout fly rod 8' (2/2)	N/A	3500	7000
Model 224 salmon fly rod 10' (3/2)	N/A	2000	4000
Model 228 heavy trout fly rod 9' (3/2)	N/A	2200	4500

GEPHART MFG.CO	poor-fair	good-vg	ex-mint
Tubular steel "Gep" fly rod 8 1/2' (2/1)	5	12	28
Tubular steel "Gep" casting rods c.1939	3	8	15
Tubular steel "Gep-Rod" auto reel-lock c.1928	4	9	18
"Actionized" solid steel casting rod 5-51/2'	4	9	18
Set of steel bait rods (2 tips) in case c.1930	10	20	40

H.S. GILLUM	poor-fair	good-vg	ex-mint
Trout fly rod made in Conn. 7' (2/2)	N/A	4200	8000
Dry fly trout rod 7 1/2' (2/2)	N/A	4000	7500
Trout fly rod 8' (2/2)	N/A	3000	5800
Trout fly rod 8 1/2' (3/2)	N/A	2500	5000
Heavy trout fly rod 8' 7" (2/2)	N/A	1900	3900
Salmon fly rod 9' (3/2)	600	1100	2000
Salmon fly rod 9 1/2' (3/2)	500	900	1800

GOODWIN GRANGER	poor-fair	good-vg	ex-mint
"Aristocrat" trout fly rod 7' (2/2)	200	400	800
"Favorite" trout fly rod 7 1/2' (3/2) c. 1930	150	300	650
"Favorite trout fly rod 8 1/2' (3/2)	90	200	400
"Victory" trout fly rod 8 1/2' (3/2)	75	175	350
"Special" trout fly rod 8' (3/2)	100	250	495
"Special" trout fly rod 8 1/2' (3/2)	80	185	365
"Special" fly rod 9' (3/2)	70	165	295
"Champion" fly rod 9' (3/2)	65	155	285
"Champion" fly rod 9 1/2' (3/2)	60	145	275
"Colorado Special" fly rod 9 1/2' (3/2) c.1926	65	150	295
"Denver Special" fly rod 9' (3/2) c.1927	75	170	325
"Premier" fly rod 9' (3/2) c.1940	70	165	300
"Premier" baitcasting rod 5' (2/1) c.1935	55	130	240
"Goodwin Granger" baitcasting rod 6' (1 piece)	50	110	215
"Granger Deluxe" baitcasting rod 6' (2/1)	55	130	240

GREAT LAKES PRODUCTS	poor-fair	good-vg	ex-mint
"Imperial" 6' casting rod with built-in reel	15	35	60

GOODALL	poor-fair	good-vg	ex-mint
"Good-All" rod with built-in reel (Ogallala, Neb.)	12	30	55

GEORGE HALSTEAD	poor-fair	good-vg	ex-mint
Trout fly rods 7 1/2 - 8' (3/2)	400	1400	2900
Trout fly rod 9' (3/2)	300	1000	2000
Salmon fly rod 9' (3/2)	200	700	1400

HARDY BROS. (England)	poor-fair	good-vg	ex-mint
"Palakona #5" trout fly rod 6' (2/1)	100	200	410
"Palakona #6" trout fly rod 7 1/2' (2/2)	125	295	550
"Palakona #7" trout fly rod 8' (2/1)	90	185	325
"Palakona #8" fly rod 8 1/2' (2/1)	80	160	275
"Palakona Deluxe" trout fly rod 8' (3/2) c.1935	95	200	395
"Phantom" trout fly rod 7' (2/1)	85	175	350
"Phantom" trout fly rod 8' (2/1)	80	160	335
"Phantom" trout fly rod 8 1/2' (2/1)	70	140	310
"Marvel" fly rod 7 1/2' (3/2) c.1926	195	400	800
"Marvel" fly rod 7 1/2' (3/2) c.1955	175	350	750
"C.C. DeFrance trout fly rod 7' (2/2)	165	325	700
"C.C. DeFrance trout fly rod 8' (2/2)	150	300	600
"C.C. DeFrance trout fly rod 9' (2/1) c.1927	100	200	400
"Fairchild" light trout fly rod 8' (3/2) c.1940	100	250	475
"Fairchild" trout fly rod 9' (3/2) c.1920	80	160	295
"The Tourney" fly rod 8' (2/1)	80	165	300
"Hollolight trout fly rod 7 1/2' ((3/2)	165	325	695
"Hollolight" trout fly rod 8' (3/2) gold parts	100	210	425
"Deluxe" fly rod 8 1/2' (3/2) bridge guides	95	195	325
"Gold Medal" salmon fly rod 9' (3/2)	75	175	310
"Gold Medal" salmon fly rod 9 1/2' (3/2)	75	150	290
"Salmon Deluxe" fly rod 8 1/2' (3/2)	75	165	295
"Kohinoor" heavy trout fly rod 8' 9" (2/1)	50	125	235
"JJ Hardy Triumph" fly rod 8' 9" (3/2) c.1935	65	165	275
"JJ Hardy Triumph" fly rod 8' 9" (2/1) c.1935	50	125	235
"Rogue River" salmon fly rod 9 1/2' (3/2) c.1950	90	200	320
"Hollokona Salmon Deluxe" fly rod 9 1/2' (3/2)	90	200	320

“Halford Knockabout” fly rod 9 1/2’ (2/1)	55	125	235
“Halford Knockabout” fly rod 10 1/2’ (2/1)	50	120	210
“Wye” salmon fly rod 10’ (3/2) screw-lock ferrules	45	100	200
“LRH” trout fly rod 9’ 4” (3/2) c.1930	60	140	275
“LRH” two handed salmon rod 14’ (3/1)	50	125	225
“Fairy-Palakona” antique fly rod 10’ (3/2) c. 1905	60	150	300
“Aydon” greenheart wood trout rod 10’ (3/2)	40	75	150
“Arjon” heavy spinning rod 7 1/2’ (2/1)	20	55	120
“Waneless 9-10 lb.” spinning rods 7’ (2/1) c.1935	25	65	135
“Waneless 9-10 lb.” spin or worming rods 10’ (2/1)	25	65	135
“Waneless 6 lb.” spinning rod 7’ (2/1) c.1935	35	75	150
“Waneless 4 lb.” spinning rod 7’ (2/1)	40	85	165
“Waneless 2 lb.” ultra-light spinning rods 7’ (2/1)	50	115	235
“Jock Scott” baitcasting rod 5 1/2’ (2 size tips) c.1955	60	125	250
“Overhead” baitcasting rod 6’ (2/1) locking ferrules	40	85	165
“Victor” casting rod 7’ (2/1)	20	70	145
“Septre” fiberglass fly rod 7 1/2’ (2/1)	15	40	75
“Fibalight Spinning - 2 lb.” fiberglass rod 6’ 2’ (2/1)	15	40	75

HIRAM HAWES	poor-fair	good-vg	ex-mint
Trout fly rod 8’ (2/2) c.1925	500	1300	2800
Trout fly rod 8 1/2’ (3/2) c.1920	450	1100	2300
Trout fly rod sold by A&F 9’ (3/2) c.1925	400	1000	2100
Salmon fly rod 9’ (3/2)	400	900	2000
Dry Fly Salmon fly rod 10’ (3/2) c.1920	225	500	1100

HEDDON	poor-fair	good-vg	ex-mint
#8 heavy trout fly rod 9’ (3/2)	40	100	190
#10 “featherweight” fly rod 7 1/2’ (2/2)	90	265	400
#10 trout fly rod 8’ (3/2)	65	160	295
#10 heavy trout fly rod 9’ (3/2) c.1955	40	100	190
#10 salmon fly rod 9’ (3/2) c.1935	40	95	180
#13 trout fly rod 7 1/2’ (2/2)	90	275	450

#13 "Lucky Angler" fly rod 8 1/2' (3/2)	50	135	225
#13 "Lucky Angler" fly rod 9' (3/2)	40	100	185
#13 "Lucky Angler" fly rod 9 1/2' (3/2)	35	85	165
#14 "Featherweight" fly rod 7 1/2' (2/2)	95	285	495
#14 "Thorobred" fly rod 8 1/2' (3/2) c.1931	55	145	235
#14 "Thorobred" heavy trout fly rod 9' (3/2)	50	115	210
#14 "Thorobred" heavy fly rod 9 1/2' (3/2)	40	95	175
#17 "Black Beauty" fly rod 7 1/2' (2/2)	100	295	500
#17 "Black Beauty" fly rod 8' (3/2)	85	225	400
#17 "Black Beauty" fly rod 8 1/2' (3/2)	75	165	300
#19 "Riptide" salmon fly rod 9' (3/2)	65	160	275
#20 "Bill Stanley" trout fly rod 8' (3/2)	85	225	395
#20 "Bill Stanley" fly rod 8 1/2' (3/2) c.1935	70	165	295
#20 "Bill Stanley" trout fly rod 9' (3/2)	60	155	250
#20 "Bill Stanley" heavy fly rod 9 1/2' (3/2)	50	145	240
#35 "Peerless" fly rod 8' (3/2) c.1932	90	235	415
#35 "Deluxe" fly rod 8 1/2' (3/2) c.1950	80	185	335
#35 "Peerless" fly rod 9' (3/2) c.1950	75	175	310
#35 "Peerless" heavy fly rod 9 1/2' (3/2) c.1932	65	165	295
#50 "Deluxe President" fly rod 8' (3/2) c.1948	95	250	435
#50 "Deluxe President" fly rod 8 1/2' (3/2)	85	210	395
#50 "President" fly rod 9' (3/2)	80	190	350
#50 "Deluxe President" fly rod 9' (3/2)	80	190	350
#50 "President" fly rod 9 1/2' (3/2)	70	165	300
#115 trout fly rod 7 1/2' (3/2)	125	300	525
#115 trout fly rod 8' (3/2)	95	275	475
#115 "Premier" fly rod 8 1/2' (3/2)	85	215	425
#125 "Expert" trout fly rod 8 1/2' (3/2)	85	225	450
#125 "Expert" trout fly rod 9' (3/2)	80	195	375
"Drueding Special" trout fly rod 7 1/2' (3/2) c.1925	120	275	500
"Marvin Hedge" bass fly rod 8' 10" (3/2)	95	200	400
Early "Dowagiac" Calcutta bait rod 5' (2/1) c.1900	50	100	200
"Dowagiac" 1908 patent bait rod 5 1/2' (2/1)	40	95	175

#1 baitcasting rod 4 1/2' (1pc) composition cork grip	15	40	75
# 1 1/2 baitcasting rod 5' (1pc) no fore grip	15	40	75
#2-A baitcasting rod 5' (1pc) cork/silver seat c.1935	20	60	100
#2 1/2 baitcasting rod 5 1/2' natural cork grips	20	55	95
#4 "Chieftain" casting rod 5' (2 pc. handle/tip) c.1932	25	65	110
#6 baitcasting rod 4 1/2' (handle/tip) c.1932	25	65	115
#9 heavy baitcasting rod 5' (handle/tip)	20	50	90
#15 baitcasting rod 5 1/2' (agate gds/nickel silver fittings)	25	70	120
#25 "Expert" casting rod 5 - 51/2' (w/extra tip c.1931)	35	80	145
#25 "Super Deluxe" casting rod 5' (chkrd. wood grip)	40	75	130
Model 200 baitcasting rod 5'	20	55	110
Model 400 baitcasting rod 5 1/2' c.1930	25	70	125
Model 600 baitcasting rod 6'	25	70	125
Model 850 R bait cast rod 6' (1piece)	25	70	125
Model 900 light trolling rod 5 1/2' (2/1)	20	55	95
Model 2500 special casting rod 5' (2/1) c. 1955	50	90	175
Model 2550 spec. casting rod 5' with walnut foregrip	50	90	175
"Jim Heddon's Favorite" baitcasting rod 5 1/2'	25	60	100
"J. Heddon's Favorite" #851 bait rod 6' (walnut grip)	35	75	135
"Reliable" bait casting rod (1 piece) detachable handle	15	45	80
Heddon Big Game trolling rod 5 1/2' agate guides	35	70	140
Heddon bamboo spinning rod 5 1/2' (2/2)	40	80	165
Heddon steel casting rod (1pc.) "bamboo" paint c.1935	10	30	60
Heddon steel salmon rod (2pc.) "bamboo" paint c.1950	10	30	60
"Hedliner" fiberglass trout fly rod 9' (2/1) c.1955	5	15	30
"Hedliner" #7105 fiberglass spinning rod 7' (2/1)	4	10	20
"Golden Mark 50" fiberglass fly rod 6'6" (2/1) c.1960	8	30	60
"Mark I" fiberglass fly rods 8-9' (2/1) c.1966	5	15	30
"Mark II" fiberglass trout fly rods 8-9' (2/1) c.1965	6	18	32
"Mark III" fiberglass fly rods 8-9' (2/1) c.1965	7	20	40
"Mark IV" fiberglass fly rods 7 1/2-9' c.1965	7	25	45
"Mark I — IV" fiberglass casting & spinning rods	3	9	18
"Pal Black Beauty" fiberglass spinning rod 6 1/2' (2/1)	8	20	45

"Lifetime Pal" fiberglass fly rods with wire guide wraps	4	10	20
"Lifetime Pal" fiberglass casting & spinning rods c.1966	3	9	18
"Pal" steel casting rod 4 to 5 1/2' (1pc.) red butt c.1935	5	20	40
"Pal" fiberglass fly rod 7 1/2' (2/1) c.1953	5	15	35
"Pal" fiberglass fly 8 1/2' (2/1) c.1955	5	15	30
"Pal" fiberglass baitcasting rod 6' (2/1)	5	15	30

J.C. HIGGINS - SEARS

	poor-fair	good-vg	ex-mint
Model 3001 trout fly rod 9' (3/2)	20	55	95
Model 3004 trout fly rod 9' (3/1)	15	40	70
Sears "Ted Williams" fiberglass fly rod 9' (2/1)	6	18	35
Fiberglass spinning rod 6 1/2' (2/1) c.1960	4	12	25

HORROCKS - IBBOTSON CO.

	poor-fair	good-vg	ex-mint
"Cascade" fly rod 8 1/2' (3/2)	20	65	110
"Cascade" fly rod 9' (3/2) c.1948	20	55	95
"Tonka Queen" fly rod 7' 9" (2/2)	35	115	195
"Tonka Prince" fly rod 7' (2/2) c.1950	30	95	175
"Pocono" trout fly rod 7' (2/1)	25	65	135
"Catskill" fly rod 9' (3/2) form case c.1920	20	55	120
"Spinner" heavy trout fly rod 9' (3/2)	20	50	85
"Spinner" trout fly rod 8 1/2' (3/2)	20	55	95
"Canada Creek" trout fly rod 8' (3/2)	25	75	135
"Governor" fly rod 9' (3/1)	15	30	70
"Lucky Ace" fly rod 8 1/2' (3/1)	15	35	75
"Hexi Super-Cane" fly rod 9' (3/2) c.1932	20	50	90
"Black River" comb. fly/baitcasting rod 8 1/2' 3/2	15	40	85
"Expert" baitcasting rod 5 1/2' (1pc.) c.1938	15	35	65
"Challenger" baitcasting rod 4' (2/1) agate guides	15	30	60
"Ontario" baitcasting rod 4 1/2' (2/1) finger grip seat	15	30	60
"Geneva" spinning rod 6 1/2' (2/1)	15	40	75
"Mohawk" #1423 fiberglass spinning rod 6 1/2'	5	13	35
"Jamaica" boat rod 5 1/2' (2/1) wood handle	12	22	55

"Skipper" boat rod 6' (2/1)	10	18	40
"100" heavy boat rod 7 1/2' (2/1)	10	20	55
"Peconic" deep sea rod 4' 3" shaft w/20" wood butt	12	25	65
"West Coast" Big Game rod 6' 8" shaft w/28" butt	18	40	95
"Model 1900" steel trolling rod	4	12	30

GARY HOWELLS

	poor-fair	good-vg	ex-mint
Trout fly rod 7' (2/2)	225	675	1100
Trout fly rod 7 1/2' (2/2)	225	675	1100
Trout fly rod 8' (2/2)	200	500	900

HURD

	poor-fair	good-vg	ex-mint
"Supercaster" steel rod & reel combo w/walnut grip	60	110	195

H.L. LEONARD

	poor-fair	good-vg	ex-mint
Model 36 trout fly rod 7 1/2 (3/2)	300	950	2000
Model 37 early "Baby Catskill" fly rod 6' (2/2)	400	1400	3000
Model 37 "Baby Catskill" fly rod 6' (2/1)	275	800	1700
Model 37H fly rod 6 1/2' (2/2)c.1970	300	850	1800
Model 37-4 fly rod 6 1/2' (2/2) c.1980	250	700	1400
Model 38L trout fly rod 7' (2/2)	350	950	1900
Model 38H trout fly rod 7' (2/2)	250	700	1400
Model 38 1/2 "Fairy Catskill" 7 1/2 (3/2) c.1929	325	850	1950
Model 39L trout fly rod 7 1/2' (2/2)	300	800	1900
Model 39H trout fly rod 7 1/2' (3/2)	250	700	1400
Model 39 "Hunt" fast action fly rod 7 1/2' (2/2)	300	850	1900
Model 40 trout fly rod 8' (2/2) c.1973	230	625	1200
Model 40 "Hunt" trout fly rod 8' (2/2)	250	700	1450
Model 40H trout fly rod 8' (2/2) c.1978	225	600	1100
Model 41DF trout fly rod 8 1/2' (3/2)	190	450	950
Model 41L trout fly rod 8 1/2' (2/2)	200	500	1000
Model 41H heavy trout fly rod 8 1/2' (2/2) c.1976	170	400	800
Model 42 "Catskill" fly rod 8 1/2' (3/2) c.1925	300	750	1600

Model 48 trout fly rod 7' (3/2) c.1955	275	700	1500
Model 48DF trout fly rod 7' (3/2) c.1935	300	850	1800
Model 49 trout fly rod 7 1/2' (3/2) modern era	250	700	1500
Model 50DF trout fly rod 8' (3/2)	225	675	1350
Model 50 "Hunt" fast action fly rod 8' (3/2) c.1982	250	700	1500
Model 50 trout fly rod 8' (3/2) c.1975	200	650	1300
Model 51H heavy trout fly rod 8 1/2' (3/2)	165	400	775
Model 51 "Registered" fly rod 9' (3/2)	150	375	750
Model 66L trout fly rod 8' (2/2)	200	650	1250
Model 66 "Registered" fly rod 8' (2/2) pre 1964	200	600	1200
Model 66H "Registered" fly rod 8' (3/2) c.1960	185	550	1100
Model 71 salmon fly rod 8 1/2' (3/2) c.1975	170	350	725
Model 76 fly rod 8' (3/2)	200	600	1200
Model 76DF fly pack rod 8' (4/2) c.1935	250	750	1400
Model 91 salmon fly rod 12' (3/2)	140	350	700
Model 4099 fly rod 8' (3/2)	200	650	1350
Model 4099 1/2 fly rod 8 1/2' (3/2) c.1972	150	400	800
Model M12 two handed salmon fly rod 12' (3/3)	140	375	700
Model 654 "Duracane" fly rod 6 1/2' (2/2) c.1975	195	475	750
Model 704 "Duracane" fly rod 7' (2/2) impregnated	195	475	750
Model 705 "Duracane" fly rod 7' (2/2)	195	475	750
Model 754 "Duracane" fly rod 7 1/2' (2/2)	175	450	700
Model 755 "Duracane" fly rod 7 1/2' (2/2)	175	450	700
Model 804 "Duracane" fly rod 8' (2/2)	175	425	675
Model 805 "Duracane" fly rod 8' (2/2)	165	425	675
Model 806 "Duracane" fly rod 8' (2/2)	150	375	600
Model 856 "Duracane" fly rod 8 1/2' (2/2)	135	300	550
Model 857 "Duracane" fly rod 8 1/2' (2/2)	135	250	500
Model 909 "Duracane salmon fly rod 9' (2/2)	100	200	400
H.L. Leonard "Fairy-Catskill" fly rod 8' (3/2) c.1920	200	500	1000
H.L. Leonard "Fairy-Catskill" fly rod 8' 2" (3/2) c.1895	180	425	900
H.L. Leonard "Petite-Catskill" fly rod 9 1/2' (3/2) c.1895	150	375	700
H.L. Leonard "Catskill" (Mills) fly rod 9 1/2' (3/2) c.1920	145	300	600

"Tournament" trout fly rod 9' (3/2) c.1930	145	300	600
"Tournament" fly rod 9 1/2' (3/2) c.1930	145	275	550
"Registered" fly rods 81/2-91/2' (3/2) patented ferrules	145	285	575
Antique "H.L. Leonard Maker" trout fly rods c.1880	400	900	1800
Early Leonard trout fly rod 10' (3/2) c.1905	175	350	650
Early Leonard salmon fly rod 11' (3/2) c.1910	125	250	495
Early baitcasting rods 5-5 1/2' (2/1) w/cloth bag	90	195	395
Model 17 baitcasting rod 5 1/2' (2/2)	95	200	400
H.L. Leonard casting rod 5 1/2' (3/2) c.1910	100	250	475
H.L. Leonard spinning rod 6' (2/1) sliding band seat	85	195	395
Leonard saltwater boat rod 6' (agate guides)	60	100	200
Leonard "Tarpon" rod 5'7" (2/2) trumpet gds. c.1920	75	165	300
Leonard fiberglass salmon/saltwater fly rod 9'(2/1)	25	50	85
"Catskill" fiberglass fly rods 7 - 8' (2/1) c.1976	40	80	165
"Rangeley" fiberglass fly rods 7 - 8' (2/1) c.1975	30	60	120
Leonard "Model 365" fiberglass fly rod 6 1/2' (2/1)	35	75	150
Leonard "Model LEF86B" glass fly rod 8 1/2' (2/1)	25	55	95

LYON & COULSON	poor-fair	good-vg	ex-mint
"Regent" fly rod by Heddon 8' (2/2)	70	160	325
"Crown" fly rod by Heddon 7 1/2' (2/2)	75	200	495
"Crown" fly rod by Heddon 9' (3/2) c.1940	60	135	275
"Imperial" fly rod by Heddon 7 1/2' (2/2)	75	200	495
"Imperial" fly rod by Heddon 9' (3/2)	65	135	275
"Captain" fly rod by Heddon 8 1/2' (3/2)	70	145	285
Spinning rod 7' (2/1)	25	65	125
Bait casting rod 6' (2/1)	40	90	165

WILLIAM MILLS & SON	poor-fair	good-vg	ex-mint
"Mills Standard" trout fly rod 8' (3/2) by Leonard	175	375	750
"Mills Standard" trout fly rod 9' (3/2) by Leonard	125	295	500
"Mills Standard early fly rod 8' (3/2) agate stripper/top	175	395	800
"Standard" antique fly rod 10' (3/2) c. 1898	100	200	400

"Standard" Henshall style bait rod 9' (3/2) c.1900	70	180	350
"Standard" baitcasting rod 6' (3/2) agate gds. c.1920	65	175	325

MILWARDS (Britain)	poor-fair	good-vg	ex-mint
"Spincraft" two-handed spinning rod 9' (2/1)	40	100	180
"Bartleet" bamboo & greenheart rod 16' (c.1918)	45	135	210
"Flymaster" trout fly rod 8' (2/2) c.1960	65	165	300

MONTAGUE ROD & REEL CO	poor-fair	good-vg	ex-mint
"Amateur" fly rod 8' (2/1)	15	50	100
"Fishkill" fly rod 7 1/2' (2/2)	40	125	265
"Fishkill" fly rod 8 1/2' (3/2)	20	75	150
"Fishkill" fly rod 9' (3/2) c. 1938	20	70	140
"Rapidan" fly rod 7 1/2' (2/2)	40	125	265
"Rapidan" fly rod 8 1/2' (3/2)	20	70	150
"Rapidan" fly rod 9' (3/2) c.1950	20	60	125
"Rapidan" fly rod 9 1/2' (3/2) c.1939	20	55	110
"Flash" fly rod 9' (3/2) wood form case c.1925	20	65	125
"Flash" fly rod 8 1/2' (3/2)	20	65	125
"Flash" fly rod 9' (3/2) c.1940	20	60	115
"Sunbeam" fly rod 9' (3/2)	20	60	115
"Sonora" fly rod 9' (3/2) c.1935	20	60	115
"Mt. Tom" fly rod 8 1/2' (3/2)	20	65	125
"Mt. Tom" fly rod 9' (3/2)	20	50	110
"Timberlake" fly rod 8 1/2' (3/2) c.1937	20	65	125
"Timberlake" fly rod 9' (3/2)	20	50	110
"Manatou" fly rod 9' (3/2) c. 1928	20	65	125
"Clipper" fly rod 8 1/2' (3/2)	20	60	120
"Clipper" fly rod 9' (3/2) c.1940	20	50	110
"Redwing" fly rod 8 1/2' (3/2) c.1940	25	80	165
"Redwing" fly rod 9' (3/2) c.1940	20	70	140
"Redwing" fly rod 9 1/2' (3/2)	20	60	125
"Flipline" fly rod 8' (3/2) c.1929	25	85	170

"Splitswitch" fly rod 8 1/2' (3/2) c.1915 form case	20	70	135
"Splitswitch" combo fly/cast rod 9' (3/2) c.1938	15	50	100
"Fishkill" combo fly/cast rod 9' (3/2) rev. handle	15	50	100
"Eel River" combo 9' fly / 6' cast rod (3/2)	15	40	85
"Rapidan" spinning rod 7' (2/1) c.1950	20	60	115
"Redwing" baitcasting rod 5' (1piece) offset grip	12	35	80
"Fishkill" casting rod 51/2' (2/1) finger hook seat	15	40	90
"Rapidan" casting rod 5' (2/1) c.1935	12	35	80
"Clipper" baitcasting rod 5 1/2' (2/1)	12	30	65
"Flash" baitcasting rod 5' (2/1)	12	30	65
"The Sagamore" early bait rod 9' (3/2) c.1915	15	50	95
"Manatou" tarpon rod hickory butt/ rattan grip c.1928	15	50	95
"Somers Point" boat rod 6' (2/1) c.1950	10	28	55
"Monterey" boat rod 6' (2/1) c.1955	10	28	55
"Stone Harbor" boat rod 6 1/2' (2/1) c.1938	10	30	60
"Off Shore" surf rod 7' (1pc.) detach. handle c.1940	10	25	50
"Swordfish" hickory wood big game rod 7' (c.1930)	25	45	90

NARMCO	poor-fair	good-vg	ex-mint
Liotta #275 bamboo bait cast rod 5 1/2' (1 piece)	40	95	195
Conolon fiberglass rods all styles (c.1960)	4	10	25

ORVIS	poor-fair	good-vg	ex-mint
C.F. Orvis fly rod 9 1/2' (3/2) wood case, 1882 patent	200	475	800
C.F. Orvis fly rod 11' (3/2) wound grip c.1890	200	475	800
C.F. Orvis fly rod 10' (3/2) round wood case c.1890	200	475	800
Orvis early fly rod 101/2' (3/2) pat. reel seat c.1908	175	350	650
"Orvis Maker" early fly rod 8 1/2' (3/2) c.1915	165	300	600
Battenkill fly rod 6 1/2' (2/2)	150	325	600
Battenkill fly rod 7' (2/2) c.1970	150	300	550
Battenkill fly rod 7 1/2' (2/2)	150	300	550
Battenkill fly rod 7 1/2' (3/2) c.1972	150	325	595
Battenkill fly rod 8' (2/2) c.1980	125	275	450

Battenkill "Pat. Pend." 8' (2/2) c.1949	125	275	450
Battenkill fly rod 8' (3/2) c.1965	135	300	500
Battenkill fly rod 8 1/2' (2/2) #9	95	200	395
Battenkill "Salmon" rod 10' (3/2)	95	195	365
"Madison" flea fly rod 6 1/2' (2/1)	95	195	360
"Madison" fly rod 7' (2/1) c.1980	100	200	375
"Madison" fly rod 7 1/2' (2/1)	100	210	375
"Madison" fly rod 8' (2/1)	95	195	365
"Manchester" fly rod 8' (2/1)	90	190	335
"Limestone Special" Battenkill 8 1/2' (2/2) #6	135	300	500
"Limestone Special" Madison grade (2/1)	95	195	375
"Wes Jordan" fly rod 7 1/2' (2/2) leather case	225	550	850
"Wes Jordan" fly rod 8' (2/2) leather case	200	475	750
"SSS" salmon fly rod 8' 9" (2/2) c.1972	120	235	400
"Shooting Star" salmon fly rod 8 1/2' (2/2)	120	225	395
"Shooting Star" salmon fly rod 9' (2/2) c.1962	120	225	395
"Superfine" fly rod 6' (1 piece) c.1960	150	400	800
"Superfine" fly rod 6 1/2' (2/2) c.1964	150	375	600
"Superfine" fly rod 7' (2/2) c.1970	150	375	600
"Superfine fly rod 7 1/2' (2/2)	150	375	600
"Ultra-Light" fly rod 5' 9" (2/1)	125	275	550
"Midge" fly rod 7 1/2' (2/2)	150	350	600
"Flea" fly rod 6 1/2' (2/2)	125	300	500
"Seven-Three" fly rod 7' (2/2) c.1973	135	325	575
"Seven-Four" fly rod 7' (3/2)	150	395	675
"Nymph" fly rod 8' (2/2)	125	300	500
"Midge-Nymph" 7 1/2 or 7' 9" (2 length tips)	135	325	550
"Mitey Mite" fly rod 5' (2/1) c.1970	125	275	525
"Model 99" fly rod 7 1/2' (2/1)	95	195	375
"Model 99" fly rod 8 1/2' (2/2) c.1955	110	235	395
"Model 99" fly rod 8' (2/1)	90	185	325
"Deluxe" fly rod 6 1/2' (2/2) c.1962	150	395	695
"Deluxe" fly rod 7' (2/2)	150	385	675

"Deluxe" fly rod 7 1/2' (2/2)	150	375	650
"Model 125" fly rod 8' (2/2) c.1981	150	350	625
"Rocky Mountain" fly rod 6 1/2' (3/2) c.1958	150	400	795
"Traveler" trout fly rod 8' (4/1) c.1963	145	395	750
"Traveler" trout fly rod 8 1/2' (4/1)	140	375	700
"Traveler" fly rod 9' (4/1)	130	300	600
"Rocky Mountain" spinning rod 6 1/2' (3/1)	80	200	395
"Rocky Mountain" fly/spin combo rod 6 1/2' (3/2)	100	250	450
"Rocky Mountain" 2 rod set (in mahogany travel case)	350	750	1300
"Rocky Mountain" 2 rod set (in vinyl travel case) c.1963	275	675	1100
"Superlight" spinning rod 5' (2/1)	75	195	350
"Superlight" spinning rod 6' (2/1)	75	195	350
"Light" spinning rod 6 1/2' (2/1)	70	150	300
"Light" spinning rod 7' (2/1)	65	145	285
"Medium" spinning rods 7 - 7 1/2' (2/1))	60	130	235
"Heavy" spinning rods 7-7 1/2' (2/1)	50	125	200
"Heavy " spinning rod 8' (2/1) c.1961	50	125	200
Bait casting rod 6' (2/1) staggered ferrule c.1955	75	175	325
Bait casting rod 5' (1 piece w/detachable handle)	70	165	295
Bait casting rod 5 1/2' (1 piece) c.1963	70	165	295
Bait casting rod 6' (1 piece) straight handle	70	165	295
Big game trolling rod (bakelite impregnated) c.1960	55	125	225
"Golden Eagle" fiberglass fly rod 6 1/2' (2/1) c.1972	20	70	125
"Golden Eagle" light fiberglass fly rod 7' (2/1)	20	65	120
"Golden Eagle" fiberglass fly rod 7 1/2' (2/1)	18	60	110
"Golden Eagle" fiberglass fly rod 8' (2/1)	18	50	95
"Golden Eagle" fiberglass fly rods 8 1/2-9' (2/1)	15	40	80
"Golden Eagle" fiberglass spin rod (with 2 tips)	15	40	80
"Fullflex" fiberglass fly rod 7-71/2' (2/1) c.1975	15	40	80
"Fullflex" fiberglass fly rod 8-8 1/2' (2/1)	12	35	75
"Fullflex" fiberglass ultra-lite spinning rod 6' (2/1)	12	30	65
"Fullflex" fiberglass spinning rods 7-8' (2/1) c.1978	10	25	45
"Fullflex " fiberglass fly/spin pack rod 7' (4/1) c.1982	12	35	70

"Orvisco" fiberglass spinning rod 6 1/2' (2/1) c.1964	9	18	40
"Orvisco" fiberglass spinning rod 7 1/2' (2/1)	9	18	40

PAYNE ROD CO.	poor-fair	good-vg	ex-mint
"Payne Model 95" fly rod 6' (2/2)	800	2000	4000
"Payne Model 96" fly rod 6 1/2' (2/2)	750	1900	3800
"Payne Model 98" fly rod 7' (2/2) c.1960	700	1700	3500
"Payne Model 100" fly rod 7 1/2' (2/2)	600	1600	3200
"Payne Model 101" fly rod 7 1/2' (2/2)	500	1400	2900
"Payne Model 102" fly rod 8' (2/2) c.1940	450	1400	2800
"Payne Model 103" fly rod 8' (2/2) c.1960	400	1300	2600
"Payne Model 104" fly rod 8 1/2' (2/2)	350	1000	1900
"Payne Model 108" fly rod 9' (3/2)	300	900	1800
"Payne Model 198 fly rod 7 1/2' (3/2) c.1950	600	1600	3200
"Payne Model 198H fly rod 7 1/2' (3/2) c.1965	600	1500	3000
"Payne Model 200" fly rod 8' (3/2)	450	1300	2700
"Payne Model 200L" fly rod 8' (3/2)	500	1400	2900
"Payne Model 201" fly rod 8' (3/2)	450	1300	2700
"Payne Model 202" fly rod 8' (3/2) c.1960	450	1300	2700
"Payne Model 202" fly rod 8' (3/2) c.1940	500	1500	3200
"Payne Model 204" fly rod 8 1/2' (3/2)	350	950	1900
"Payne Model 205" fly rod 8 1/2' (3/2)	350	950	1900
"Payne Model 208" fly rod 9' (3/2)	300	700	1300
"Payne Model 208 H" bass fly rod 9' (3/2)	250	650	1200
"Payne Model 223" salmon fly rod 11 1/2' (3/2)	250	650	1200
"Payne Model 310" salmon fly rod 9'3" (3/2)	250	650	1200
"E.F. Payne" early trout rod 10' (3/2) c.1905	160	350	600
"E.F. Payne Special" fly rod 8 1/2' (3/2) c.1925	200	700	1400
"Payne" salmon fly rod 9' (3/2)	200	500	1000
"Payne" spinning rod 7' (2/1)	100	295	495
"Payne" medium (302M) bait rod 5 1/2' (2/2)	150	310	550
"Payne" light baitcasting rod 5 1/2' (2/2) c.1939	165	350	600

RUSS PEAK	poor-fair	good-vg	ex-mint
Zenith fiberglass fly rods c.1960	75	160	295
Zenith or Peer graphite fly rods	100	225	395

PEZON & MICHEL (France)	poor-fair	good-vg	ex-mint
Ritz “Loire” fly rod 7’ 2” (2/1) c.1970	75	175	335
Ritz “Super-Parabolic” fly rod 7’2” (2/2) c.1965	135	295	525
Ritz “Parabolic” fly rod 8’ 2” (2/1) staggered ferrule	70	165	325
Ritz “Fario Club” 8’ 5” (2/2) staggered ferrule	135	295	525
Ritz “Super-Parabolic” fly rod 8 ‘ 3” (2/2) c.1970	120	275	500
“Parabolic” fly rod 8’ 8” (2/1)	70	155	300
“Parabolic Royale” fly rod 7’ 9” (2/1)	85	195	395
Sawyer “Nymph-Parabolic” fly rod 9’ (2/2)	100	225	400
Pezon et Michel salmon fly rod 9’ (3/1) c.1970	50	130	235
Ritz “Vari-Power” fly rod 6’ (glass butt & bamboo tip)	40	95	195
Pezon et Michel ultra-light spinning rod 5’ (2/1)	55	140	245
Pezon et Michel “Elite” spinning rod 7’ (2/1)	50	135	235
“Luxor-Precision 500” spinning rod 7’ 2” (2/1)	40	110	200

PFLUEGER	poor-fair	good-vg	ex-mint
“Rocky River” baitcasting rod 5’ (1 piece)	45	95	185
“Silver Lake” baitcasting rod 5’ (2/1) c.1941	50	100	195
“Four Bros. Rivlake” bait rod 5’ (1 pc.)	20	50	90
“Goodyear” fly rod 9’ (3/2) intermediate wraps	65	135	245
“Four Bros. Dazie fly rod 9’ (3/2) c.1939	40	85	165
“Saltaire” ocean rods 6 1/2 to 7’ (detachable butt)	25	55	100

PHILLIPSON	poor-fair	good-vg	ex-mint
“Peerless” fly rod 7’ (2/2) c.1964	100	350	600
“Peerless” fly rod 7 1/2’ (2/2) c.1970	100	325	575
“Peerless” fly rod 8’ (2/2) impregnated c.1968	95	275	485
“Peerless” pack fly rod 8’ (3/2) impregnated	95	275	485
“Smuggler” pack fly rod 7’8” (4/2) c.1952	100	345	595

"Premium" fly rod 8 1/2' (3/2) hammer grip	75	185	325
"Premium" fly rod 9' (3/2) hammer grip	70	165	295
"Preferred" fly rod 8' (3/2) impregnated	90	210	385
"Pacemaker" fly rod 8' (3/2)	90	195	375
"Pacemaker" fly rod 8 1/2' (3/2)	75	175	310
"Pacemaker" fly rod 9' (3/2)	65	145	265
"Paragon" fly rod 8 1/2' (3/2)	75	175	310
"PowerPakt" fly rod 7 1/2' (2/2)	100	295	500
"PowerPakt" fly rod 8' (2/2)	90	235	395
"PowerPakt" fly rod 9' (3/2) c.1955	70	165	295
"Dry Fly Special" fly rod 8 1/2' (3/2)	75	175	310
"Haywood Zephyr" spin/fly rod 7' (2/1)	60	135	245
"Pacemaker" spinning rod 7' (2/1) c.1960	35	95	195
"Pacific" steelhead casting rod 9' (2/1)	35	90	185
"Preferred" bait casting rod 6' (impregnated)	40	95	200
"Epoxite" fiberglass midge fly rod 6 1/2' (2/2)	30	80	140
"Epoxite" fiberglass midge fly rod 7' (2/2)	30	80	140
"Epoxite" fiberglass fly rod 8' (3/2) c.1970	25	70	125
"Epoxite" fiberglass fly rod 9' (2/2) c.1972	20	50	90
"P76F" fiberglass fly rod 7 1/2' (2/1) silver ferrules	25	60	110
"Royal" fiberglass fly rod 7 1/2' (2/1) silver ferrules	25	60	110
"Royal" fiberglass fly rod 8 1/2' (2/1) silver ferrules	20	50	95
"The Scout" fiberglass fly rod 7 1/2' (2/1)	25	60	110
"Challenger" fiberglass fly/spin rod 7' (2/1)	10	40	75
"Pixie" fiberglass spin rod 7 1/2' (2/1)	9	30	60
"Expert" fiberglass spinning rod 7' (2/1)	8	25	50
"Johnson" fiberglass fly/spin rod 6' (2/1) c.1963	10	40	75
"Regal Lancer" fiberglass salmon rod 9' (2/1)	10	35	70

E.C.POWELL	poor-fair	good-vg	ex-mint
Steelhead fly rod 9' (2/2) semi-hollow, B-taper	150	425	775
Steelhead fly rod 9 1/2' (2/2) Semi-hollow	150	400	725
Steelhead fly rod 9 1/2' (3/2) semi-hollow, B-taper	150	400	725

Trout fly rod 9' (2/2)	160	435	800
Trout fly rod 8' (2/2) semi-hollow, B-taper	170	495	950
Trout fly rod 7 1/2' (2/2)	190	575	1000
Bait casting rod 6' (2/1)	85	160	300
Walton Powell trout fly rod 8' 3" (3/2)	150	425	795
Walton Powell steelhead fly rod 9' (3/2)	150	400	750

L. M. RICHARDSON	poor-fair	good-vg	ex-mint
"Peerless" tubular steel fly/cast rod 8 1/2' (4/1)	4	10	25
"Brookside" tubular steel bait rod 5' (2/1) c.1930	4	10	20
Tubular steel fly/cast rod reversible handle (c.1925)	4	10	20

JIM SCHAAF	poor-fair	good-vg	ex-mint
Browntone trout fly rod 7' (2/2)	140	400	750
Trout fly rod 7 1/2' (2/2)	140	380	700
Tournament fly rod 8' (2/2) staggered ferrule	135	350	650
"Dickerson style" Model 7013 fly rod 7' (2/2)	200	650	1250

EDGAR SEALEY (England)	poor-fair	good-vg	ex-mint
"Octopus" fly rods 8 1/2-9' (2/1) cloth bag c.1960	55	125	215

SHAKESPEARE	poor-fair	good-vg	ex-mint
Model 1233 B dry fly midge rod 6 1/2' (2/2)	100	295	475
Model 1233 trout fly rod 7 1/2' (2/2) c.1947	85	200	390
Model 1300 B-9 fly rod 9' (3/2) c.1930	30	80	150
Model 1300 fly rod 9' (3/2)	20	70	125
Model 1305 "Triumph" trout fly rod 8 1/2' (3/2)	25	75	140
Model 1308 "Premier" trout fly rod 9' (3/2) c.1940	25	75	140
Model 1312 "Tony Accetta" fly rod 9' (3/2)	35	90	175
Model 1315 B fly rod 9' (3/2) c.1935	35	85	165
Model 1326 fly rod 9' (3/2) c.1950	20	65	115
Model 1330 B fly rod 8 1/2' (3/2) c.1935	35	90	175
Model 1338 B trout fly rod 8 1/2' (3/2) c.1935	45	110	225

Model 1358 fly rod 8 1/2' (3/2) c.1950	25	70	135
Model 1360 "Silver Creek" fly rod 8 1/2' (3/2)	25	70	135
Model 1362 "Springbrook" fly rod 8 1/2' (3/2)	25	70	135
Model 1362 fly rod 9' (3/2)	20	65	115
Bait casting rod 5 1/2' (2/1) c.1950	15	45	85
"Kalamazoo" bait casting rod 5' (2/1) c.1927	20	60	100
"Tony Accetta" bait casting rod 5' (1pc.)	18	55	95
Tubular steel bait casting rods (3/1) c.1930	9	25	50
"Wonderod" FY-500A fiberglass fly rod 8 1/2' (2/1)	6	18	45
"Wonderod Purist" FY955 fiberglass fly rod 7 1/2' (2/1)	9	30	60
"Wonderod" B-814 fiberglass trout rod 8 1/2' (2/1)	7	20	55
"Wonderod" FY300 fiberglass fly rod 8 1/2' (2/1) c.1965	6	18	45
"Wonderod" 1280B fiberglass trout rod 7'9" (2/1)	7	20	55
"Wonderod" FYA250 fiberglass trout rod 7' 9" (2/1) c.1971	6	18	45
"Wonderod" FY600 fiberglass wood grain fly rod 7' (2/1)	7	20	55
"Wonderod" FY600 glass wood grain 8 1/2' (2/1) c,1971	7	20	50
"Wonderod" fly/spin combination 7' (2/1)	6	15	40
"Wonderod" SP999 pack rod 7' (7/1) c.1970	6	15	40
"Wonderod" SP921 ultra-light glass spin rod 5'(2/1)	6	15	40

J.S. SHARPE (Scotland)	poor-fair	good-vg	ex-mint
"Scottie" fly rod 7' (2/1) impregnated c.1975	60	165	275
"Scottie" featherweight fly rod 7 1/2' (2/1)	60	165	275
"Scottie" fly rod 8' (2/1) in cloth bag only	50	145	250
"Scottie" fly rod 8 1/2' (2/1) in cloth bag	40	130	210
"Spinning rod" 8' (2/1) c.1960 impregnated	35	90	175

OGDEN SMITH (England)	poor-fair	good-vg	ex-mint
Trout fly rod 7 1/2' (2/2) blued ferrules	80	225	440
Double built fly rod 8 1/2' (2/2)	60	130	245
"Warrior" trout fly rod 8' (2/1)	50	125	225
"Warrior" double built spin/fly pack rod 8 1/2' (4/2)	75	180	395
Spinning rod 6' 10" (2/1)	20	55	110

SOUTH BEND	poor-fair	good-vg	ex-mint
Model #12 fly rod 8 1/2' (3/2) c.1932	40	95	185
Model #13 fly rod 9' (3/2) c.1932	35	80	150
Model #23 fly rod 9' (3/2)	35	80	150
Model #24 fly rod 8 1/2' (3/2)	35	90	165
Model #25 "Sport Oreno" 7 1/2' (2/2) c.1935	45	145	265
Model #30 fly rod 8 1/2' (3/2) c.1931	40	100	195
Model #31 fly rod 9' (3/2) c.1931	35	85	160
Model #46 trout fly rod 8 1/2' (3/2) c.1940	40	100	195
Model #47 fly rod 9' (3/2)	35	80	150
Model #51 fly rod 8 1/2' (2/2)	40	95	175
Model #57 fly rod 8 1/2' (3/2)	35	90	165
Model #59 fly rod 8 1/2' (3/2) c.1950	35	90	165
Model #77 fly rod 9' (3/2)	35	80	150
Model #290 fly rod 7 1/2' (2/2) c.1950	40	125	225
Model #291 fly rod 7 1/2' (4/1)	40	110	200
Model #323 fly rod 8 1/2' (3/2)	35	90	165
Model #346 fly rod 9' (3/2) c.1955	35	80	150
Model #357 fly rod 8 1/2' (3/2)	35	90	165
Model #359 fly rod 8 1/2' (3/2) c.1950	35	90	165
Model #469 spin/fly rod 7' (2/1)	25	60	110
"Cross Double Built" fly rod 9' (3/2) c.1935	40	100	185
"Cross Double Built Model 155" fly rod 9' (3/2)	40	100	180
"Cross Double Built Model 166" fly rod 9' (3/2)	40	100	180
"Cross Double Built Model 264" fly rod 8 1/2' (3/2)	45	125	200
"Cross Double Built Model 266" fly rod 9' (3/2) c.1950	40	100	185
Model #4 light bait casting rod 5' (2/1) c.1932	25	45	95
Model #9 light bait casting rod 6' (2/1) c.1930	25	45	95
Model #22 bait casting rod 4 1/2' (2/1)	15	35	75
Model #62L bait casting rod 5 1/2' (2/1)	20	40	85
Early steel casting rod (4/1) screw-collar ferrule c.1925	10	30	50
"Payne" fiberglass fly rod 8' (2/1) wood reel seat	50	100	195
#3386 fiberglass fly rod 8 1/2' in wood case c.1965	35	65	125

#1166 fiberglass casting rod 6 1/2' in wood case	25	40	80
#2270 fiberglass spin rod 7' in wood case c.1965	25	40	75

F.E. THOMAS ROD CO.

F.E. THOMAS ROD CO.	poor-fair	good-vg	ex-mint
"Browntone" trout fly rod 8' (3/2) c.1925	250	650	1200
"Browntone" heavy trout fly rod 9' (3/2)	160	300	600
"Browntone" fly rod 9 1/2' (3/2) c.1925	150	295	550
"Salmon Dry Fly" rod 9 1/2' (3/2)	140	275	450
"Dirigo" trout fly rod 8' (3/2)	190	475	900
"Dirigo" trout fly rod 8 1/2' (3/2) c.1920	175	395	700
"Dirigo" trout fly rod 8 1/2' (3/2) c.1940	170	350	675
"Dirigo" fly rod 9' (3/2)	150	285	460
"Dirigo" salmon fly rod 10' (3/2)	110	230	395
"Special" pack trout fly rod 7' (3/2) c.1940	400	1000	2000
"Special" light trout fly rod 7 1/2' (2/2)	400	1100	2200
"Special" light trout fly rod 8' (2/2)	300	850	1500
"Special Fairy" light fly rod 8' (3/2)	300	875	1600
"Special" trout fly rod 8 1/2' (3/2)	170	375	725
"Special" heavy trout fly rod 9' (3/2) c.1938	160	300	575
"Bangor" trout fly rod 8 1/2' (3/2)	170	350	650
"Streamer" trout fly rod 9' (3/2)	190	460	850
"V L & D" Thomas/Edwards (c.1898) rods 9' (3/2)	200	500	950
F.E. Thomas 2 handed salmon fly rod 12' (3/2)	125	260	450
"Special" early bait casting rod 6' w/rattan grip c.1900	65	150	275
"Special" bait casting rod 6' (2/2) c.1915	95	235	395
Ocean rod 6 1/2' (1 piece w/detachable handle) c.1918	100	225	375
"Special" light trolling rod 8 1/2' (3/2)	110	240	410
"Dirigo" boat rod 8' (3/2) tunnel guides	75	170	300

THOMAS & THOMAS

THOMAS & THOMAS	poor-fair	good-vg	ex-mint
"Midge" fly rod 7 1/2' (2/2)	250	575	950
"Specialist" fly rod 7 1/2' (3/2) c.1985	250	575	950
"Paradigm" fly rod 8' (2/2) c.1980	200	550	900

"Hendrickson" fly rod 8' (2/2)	200	550	900
"Montana" fly rod 8 1/2' (2/2)	190	475	800
"Classic" fly rod 6 1/2' (2/1) c.1982	160	375	595
"Classic" fly rod 7' (2/2) early varnish c.1972	175	400	695
"Classic" fly rod 7 1/2' (2/1)	160	375	595
"Classic" fly rod 8' (2/1) impregnated	150	325	495
"Custom Baitcast" 5 1/2' (2/1) c.1975	100	235	385

TRUE TEMPER

	Poor-fair	good-vg	ex-mint
Solid steel bait casting rods (1925- 40) vinyl case	4	9	17

EDWARD K. TRYON CO.

	poor-fair	good-vg	ex-mint
"Kingfisher" fly rod by Montague 7 1/2' (3/2)	40	125	245
"Kingfisher " fly rod by Montague 8' (3/2) c.1935	40	110	215
"Kingfisher" fly rod by Montague 9' (3/2)	35	70	140
"Jay Harvey" fly rod by Heddon 9' (3/2) c.1930	45	115	200
"Kingfisher - Lincoln" fly rod 8 1/2' (3/2) Heddon	45	125	235

UNION HARDWARE

	poor-fair	good-vg	ex-mint
Trout fly rod 8 1/2' (2/2)	35	80	145
Bass fly rod 9' (3/2)	30	70	120
Trolling rod 8' (3/2) c.1930	20	45	85
"Sunnybrook" 4 piece steel rod w/ detachable handle	6	15	30
"Sampson" steel casting rod 8 1/2' (3/1)	6	15	30
Tubular steel bait casting rod 5 1/2' (3/1)	6	15	30
Tubular steel fly rod 9 1/2' (3/2) c.1915	7	20	40
Telescoping Steel fly/casting rods c.1925	6	15	30

NAT USLAN

	poor-fair	good-vg	ex-mint
Trout fly rod 7' (2/2) 5 bamboo strips	150	375	600
"Deluxe" trout fly rod 7 1/2' (3/2) c.1955	165	395	650
"Spencer" fly rod 8' (2/2) 5-sided	100	250	495
"Spencer" fly rod 8 1/2' (2/2) 5-sided	90	235	450

Salmon fly rod 9' (3/2)	60	150	300
"Spencer" spinning rod 7' (2/1)	35	85	165
"Airex" spinning rods 6' (2/1)	35	85	165

U.S. NET & TWINE CO.	poor-fair	good-vg	ex-mint
"Kosmic" fly rod 10' (3/2) c.1890 flip-ring guides	400	1000	2200

EDWARD VOM HOFE	poor-fair	good-vg	ex-mint
Trout fly rod by Heddon 8 1/2' (3/2) c.1940	100	230	425
Light Salmon fly rod by Payne 9' 3/2	200	450	850
Salmon fly rod by Edwards 9' 9" (3/2)	75	185	375
Two Handed salmon fly rod 12' (3/2) c.1925	65	150	300
Bait rod 5 1/2' (1 pc.) detach handle c.1910	80	200	395
Early boat rod 10' (7 strip bamboo) rattan grip c.1885	180	375	650
Ocean trolling rod 5' with 18" rattan handle c.1915	60	175	325
Greenheart wood boat rod 6' (dual agate guides)	50	125	250
Hickory wood ocean rod (No.6) 5 1/2' c.1900	55	145	285

WEBER	poor-fair	good-vg	ex-mint
Trout fly rod by Heddon 7 1/2' (3/2)	80	210	395
Trout fly rod by Heddon 8' (3/2)	70	185	350
"Jock Scott" fly rod by Heddon 9' (3/2)	40	100	195
"Deschutes Special" fly rod by Heddon 9' (3/2)	40	100	195
"Henshall Special" fly rod by Edwards 8 1/2' (3/2)	65	145	300

JOHN WEIR & SON	poor-fair	good-vg	ex-mint
Trout fly rods 8' (2/2)	95	300	595
Bait casting rods 6' (1 piece) w/detach handle	75	165	300

WINCHESTER	poor-fair	good-vg	ex-mint
Model 6044 trout fly rod 8' (3/2) c.1932	75	200	385
Model 6085 fly rod 9' (3/2) c.1932	60	140	275
"Armax" brand fly rod 9' (3/2) c.1935	50	110	200

“Armax” brand casting rod 5 1/2’ (2/2)	30	70	125
Model 6405 light bait casting rod 5 1/2’ (2/1) c.1928	40	100	195
Model 6340 bait rod 5’ (2/1) agate guides c.1928	35	90	175
Telescopic steel fly/bait rod 9’ with reversible handle	20	50	100
Tubular steel bait casting rod 4 1/2’ (4/1) c.1930	20	45	95
Solid steel bait casting rod 3 1/2’ (2/1) c.1930	15	40	80

WINSTON	poor-fair	good-vg	ex-mint
Trout fly rod 8’ (2/2) made in S.F. California c.1965	200	550	1000
Trout fly rod 8’ (2/1) original with 1 tip circa 1965	165	400	700
Trout fly rod 8 1/2’ (2/2) Calif. “Hollowbuilt”	200	550	1000
Steelhead fly rod 9’ (2/1) early Stoner built c.1950	150	395	695
Tournament fly rod 9 1/2’ (2/1) c.1955	150	395	695
“R.L. Winston” trout fly rod 7’ (2/2) Montana	200	500	900
“R.L. Winston Leetle Feller” fly rod 7’ (2/1)	150	345	600
“R.L. Winston” fly rod 7 1/2 (2/2) Montana c.1985	200	495	875
“R.L. Winston” trout fly rod 8’ (2/2)	200	475	825
Winston “Lagoon” drift rod 9’ (2/1) c.1960	100	235	445
Winston baitcasting rod 7’ (2/1) early Stoner built	90	195	395

WRIGHT & MCGILL (Granger)	poor-fair	good-vg	ex-mint
“Aristocrat” fly rod 7’ (2/2)	175	450	775
“Aristocrat” fly rod 7 1/2’ (3/2)	145	395	700
“Aristocrat” fly rod 8 1/2’ (3/2)	90	210	395
“Aristocrat” fly rod 9’ (3/2)	75	185	345
“Champion” fly rod 9’ (3/2)	70	175	285
“Victory” fly rod 7’ (2/2)	130	375	600
“Victory” fly rod 8 1/2’ (3/2)	75	180	335
“Victory” fly rod 9’ (3/2)	70	165	285
“Special” fly rod 8 1/2’ (3/2)	85	185	375
“Special” fly rod 9’ (3/2) c. 1950	70	170	325
“Favorite” fly rod 8’ (3/2)	90	235	400
“Favorite” fly rod 9’ (3/2)	70	165	310

"Stream & Lake" fly rod 8 1/2' (3/2)	75	180	335
"Stream & Lake" fly rod (9050) 9' (3/2)	70	170	325
"Granger Deluxe" fly rod 8 1/2' (3/2)	75	175	345
"Waterseal" impregnated fly rod 8 1/2' (3/2)	70	165	300
"Special" spin/fly combo rod 8' (3/2)	60	135	250
"Special" spin/fly combo rod 8 1/2' (3/2(	55	125	235
"Special" baitcasting rod 5 1/2' (2/1)	40	95	185
"Paramount" baitcasting rod 6' (2/1)	35	90	175
"All American" fiberglass fly rod 8 1/2' (2/1) c.1952	10	30	65
"All American" fiberglass spinning rod 7 1/2'	8	18	40
"President" fiberglass pack fly rod 8' (4/1) c.1958	9	28	50

PAUL YOUNG	poor-fair	good-vg	ex-mint
"Midge" trout fly rod 6' 3" (2/2)	400	1200	2400
"Driggs" trout fly rod 7' 2" (2/2) c.1960	400	1200	2300
"Perfectionist" trout fly rod 7 1/2' (2/2) c.1960	400	1200	2300
"Martha Marie" trout fly rod 7 1/2' (2/2)	400	1100	2200
"Parabolic 15" trout fly rod 8' (2/2)	300	900	1900
"Parabolic 16" trout fly rod 8 1/2' (2/2) c.1950	275	750	1400
"Parabolic 17" fly rod 8 1/2' (2/2) c.1955	250	650	1300
"Texas General" heavy fly rod 8 1/2' (2/2)	225	575	1100
"Ace" trout fly rod 7 1/2' (3/2)	175	395	600
"Ace" fly rod 8' (2/2) blank not made by Young	150	295	500
"Bobby Doerr" salmon fly rod 9' (2/2)	190	400	800
"Spin Master" spinning rod 7' (2/1)	95	225	450
Spin/Fly combination rod 8' (2/2) c.1958	235	600	1100
Casting rod 6' (1 piece) medium action	75	185	375
Casting rod 6 1/2' (2/1) staggered ferrule c.1942	90	215	400
Saltwater spinning rod 9' (2/1) foulproof guides	65	160	295

COLLECTING TRENDS & VALUATION NOTES (3rd Printing)

Values of quality fiberglass rods have increased 30 - 40%, particularly those in excellent or better condition. Bamboo fly rod values generally advanced 10 - 20%, and restorable cane rods of all types in "fair" or "good" condition increased an average of 25%. These changes can be factored-in to determine current, rough estimate of worth. Be aware that incredible prices are occasionally realized at on-line auction sites where condition and scarcity are often exaggerated.